brewing with
WHEAT

The 'Wit' and 'Weizen' of World Wheat Beer Styles

by Stan Hieronymus

Brewers Publications
A Division of the Brewers Association
PO Box 1679, Boulder, Colorado 80306-1679
www.BrewersAssociation.org

Printed in the United States of America.

10 9 8 7 6 5 4 3 2 1

ISBN: 0-937381-95-0
ISBN-13: 978-0-937381-95-3

Library of Congress Cataloging-in-Publication Data

Hieronymus, Stan.
  Brewing with wheat : the "wit' and weizen" of world wheat beer styles / by
Stan Hieronymus.
      p. cm.
  Includes bibliographical references and index.
  ISBN 978-0-937381-95-3
  1. Wheat beer. 2. Brewing. I. Title.

  TP577.H464 2010
  641.2'3--dc22
      2009048851

Publisher: Kristi Switzer
Technical Editor: Ashton Lewis
Copy Editing and Index: Daria Labinsky
Production and Design Management: Stephanie Johnson
Cover and interior design: Julie Korowotny
Cover Photography by Jon Edwards Photography and ©iStockphoto.com/
Valentin Casarsa
Special thanks to Sahm and Boelter for the glassware provided for the cover
photos.
Interior Photos: Stan Hieronymus unless otherwise noted.

*To the memory of Michael Jackson, because
all books that would broaden what we know about
beer should be so dedicated until further notice.*

TABLE OF CONTENTS

ACKNOWLEDGEMENTS

My advice to anybody writing a book is to start with a group of people to help you who are as generous as those in the brewing community, and then line up the best copy editor you can find. I would not have started this project had I not known my fastidious wife, Daria Labinsky, would be at the end to help make sense of what I wrote. She and our daughter, Sierra, are the best traveling companions a man could wish for. Thank you, Sierra, for spending part of your birthday at Bayerischer Bahnhof Gasthaus and Gose Brauerei in Leipzig, not a dream location for most girls turning twelve.

Dan Carey of New Glarus Brewing likened me to the television detective Columbo. "You are leaving, then there is always one more question," he said. I am particularly grateful to all those who answered the extra questions. There are far too many to list, but the particularly patient included Carey, Hans-Peter Drexler, Eric Toft, Steven Pauwels, and Jason Perkins.

To write about these beers requires understanding the history behind them and the culture surrounding them, not a slam dunk for an

American who grew up in central Illinois and struggled with high school German. Were it not for the generosity of Ron Pattinson and Yvan De Baets this would be a much lesser book technically and culturally. Martyn Cornell, Carl Miller, Derek Walsh, Bob Hansen, Don Bechtel, and Gordon Strong further helped in matters related to history and brewing science.

Thanks to the brewers who contributed recipes: Jean-François Gravel, Bill Aimonetti, Todd Ashman, Pauwels, and Kristen England. And double thanks to England for additional insights.

The final step, producing a book, was made easier by Kristi Switzer, who took the reins at Brewers Publications from Ray Daniels, and Julie Korowotny. I sleep much better at night because Ashton Lewis agreed to be the technical editor, and particularly value the suggestions he made to make the book more understandable.

I can't overstate my appreciation for everything Yvan De Baets contributed, including the Foreword, but also all the work he put into the third chapter at a time when he was busy getting his own brewery going. It's not easy keeping the brewing world honest, but he's doing more than his share.

FOREWORD

When my friend Stan asked me to participate in his new book, I had two reactions. The first one was pride. Being asked to contribute to the work of such a knowledgeable beer writer is definitely something! The second was: "Wheat beers? How boring!" Indeed, if the German *weizens* are without a doubt a fascinating style, and if it is really easy to find plenty of exquisite examples of them, the same is certainly not true with their Belgian or "Belgian-like" counterparts. Far from that. In my country, wheat beers (*witbieren* in Dutch, *bières blanches* in French) have been considered as a sort of commodity for a few decades. The big boys have to have one in their range, with as their main target the people "who don't like beer so much" and the women (yes, a lot of brewers still have outdated macho views of their own customers). And, as always, a lot of small brewers just imitate them. In turn all those are then often imitated by foreign brewers. As a result, and even if very nice examples do exist, far too many of the white beers to be found around the world are sweetish coriander soups resembling spicy lemonade with some alcohol in it.

Yet, white beers, and, more generally, wheat beers, were once something else in Belgium. And digging into the past shows a fantastic variety of fascinating styles. To correctly understand the picture, one has to keep in mind that, in the past in Belgium, wheat was certainly as important as barley in beer brewing. When talking about the general characteristics of Belgian brewing, local doctor Jean-Baptiste Vrancken wrote that in Belgium almost all the beers, even the ones called Orge (barley), contained 50 percent wheat. He added that when a Belgian brewer wanted to make a stronger beer, he won't add more barley *and* wheat, but wheat *only*. Indeed, in the old books, one can find an impressive list of old Belgian styles containing that cereal, and this without even counting the classical trio Louvain's (or Leuven's) white, Hoegaerden, and Peeterman. Name it: *Brune de Malines, Saison de Liège, Bière de Ath, Grisette, Orge d'Anvers, Seef* (Antwerp's White), *Lambic de Bruxelles, Bière de Diest, Caves de Lierre, Bière de Putte, Bière de Tirlemont, Bière de Jodoigne, Bière de Bois-le-Duc, Saison de Wallonie* (eventually), *Brune & Blanche du Pays Wallon,* etc. And there were more! The reasons? According to Vrancken, wheat imparts smoothness and *bouquet.*

But let another Belgian tell his version: Wheat was there, grown anyway for the making of bread, and because it didn't have to undergo a malting process it was cheaper than malted barley. Yes, the Belgians love to drink, but they are also pragmatic people. Another consideration has to be added, though: Until the end of the nineteenth century, the brewers strongly believed that the use of wheat helped the beer to keep longer (even if the classical whites had a very short shelf life). Maybe this is related to the "strength" bread gives to human bodies? It reminds us anyway that, as the histories of beer and bread are so closely related, it is more than probable that wheat was used for making beer since beer has existed. It is now proven that wheat *and* barley are at the origin of civilisation, as they wanted to be supplied all the year round—which demanded they cultivate them. Was it for bread or for beer? Some extremely serious paleo-anthropologists strongly believe it was for the latter, which, by the way, would make beer one of the keystones that permitted civilisation to be born—nothing less!

Tracking those old beers—German, Belgian, whatever—makes one realize that the key to the old styles, probably even more than the recipes themselves, was to be found in the local microflora of each brewery. Vrancken reports eighteenth and nineteenth century trials, in which brewmasters were sent from a brewery to another similar one, with all their equipment, raw material, and techniques. Sometimes the grains were even crushed in the first brewery to mimic the process perfectly. They never succeeded in making the same beer in the next village! Mixed fermentation was the norm, with local consortia of yeasts and bacteria working in a beautiful symbiosis.

The old-fashioned Belgian wheat beers, and more than likely German ones as well, were obviously a complex, rich, and healthy beverage. Due to their mixed fermentation with lactic acid bacteria, they were probably very interesting for the intestine flora, acting as *pro*biotics. With their low attenuation, they were rich in mid- and long-chain carbohydrates, providing a long-term energy source and probably acting as *pre*biotics. Wheat itself, and poorly modified malted barley, introduced nitrogen compounds to the body. They also contained less harmful by-products like alcohol and kilning products, because their alcohol content was around 2.5 to 3 percent and the malt was wind-dried. It is so true that Hendrik Verlinden, in 1933, didn't hesitate to compare them with *kephir, koumiss, mazun, yogurts, lebenraib*, etc., all making a welcome comeback as health food today.

This indicates that most of the modern white beer makers are not only missing the fun of those crazy fermentations, but also, probably, an interesting market. But it shows also that an old-fashioned nineteenth century Hoegaerden, for instance, with its spontaneous fermentation, strong lactic acid presence, and richness in complex sugars probably resembled some precursors of what we would recognize as "beer" today, which Ian Hornsey calls "fossil beer" in *A History of Beer and Brewing*, naming for instance the *braga* of Eastern Europe, made with millet, or the *kvass*, of Eastern Europe and Russia, made with rye.

By the way, I'm asking myself how a company could ever trademark a name like Hoegaarden, which was a style of beer once made by many breweries. The same applies for another beer made with wheat: *Grisette*. The shameful thing is that those beers have little—nothing in the case of the second—in common with the original styles they refer to. These should be names available to any brewer. Imagine if Guinness would have done that with "Stout"!

For a modern brewer it is indeed funny to see that the key to a style resides in what is now considered the Evil in our breweries: lactic acid bacteria! I recently went to help a local brewery in France having huge infection problems. Funnily enough their White, which otherwise was a bland, overly spicy, cloying stuff, became a thirst quenching, complex beer after it was infected. I cured the problem, but was a little sad, as these little microorganisms had undoubtedly performed an unrewarded great job.

Thanks to Stan, and the research I had to do, I have now decided to make my own White at de la Senne. Honestly, I would have never thought I ever would. Might this book cause you to feel like making one, too!

Yvan De Baets
Brewer
Brasserie de la Senne
Brussels, Belgium

INTRODUCTION

"The wheat beer makes friends everywhere. You look to the Chinese people; you give them a wheat beer and they are happy like Christmas."
— Matthias Schneider, Private Brauereigasthof Schneider

October 7, 2008. Not many hours after he has finished pouring beer for late night customers in the small bar at the front of the Weissbräu Freilassing hotel, owner Bernard Kuhn begins his morning by sanitizing flip-top bottles in the tiny brew house in the back. Today he will package a batch of *hefeweizen* he brewed using wood-fired copper kettles, fermented in open vats, and is about to bottle condition with traditional *speise*, much like his mother and father did when they bought the brewery in 1968.

Kuhn was ten years old when he began helping his parents, both trained brewers, in the family business. As all German brewers must, he later underwent much more formal training, working at various breweries and attending technical school, sandwiching in a stint in the army.

Many Americans, including professional brewers and beer tourists, stay at Weissbräu Freilassing, in part because the town of Freilassing is located near Salzburg, Austria, and the commuter bus stops just around the corner. It's the oldest *weissbier* brewery in the region, having opened in 1910, long before wheat beers became fashionable in the 1970s.

The copper kettles date from the 1950s and were coal-fired until the 1970s. "The neighbors didn't much like the coal," says Kuhn, who bought the brewery and hotel from his family in 2008. Although using wood may sound romantic, these are not handsome logs cut from nearby forests. Recycled wood—from used shipping pallets, for instance—shares space in the narrow alley behind the brewery with plastic crates filled with returnable flip-tops.

The kettles could hold 22 hectoliters each, but Kuhn brews in batches of 14 to 15 hectoliters (12.5 barrels), using a decoction mash if necessary, transferring the wort into a separate room with two open fermenters. He refreshes his yeast about every six months, getting a new batch from another brewery. He produces a modest 500 to 700 hectoliters annually (600 barrels in a busy year), most of it *hefeweizen*. The brewery began selling the *hefe* in kegs only in 1994, adding a *dunkelweizen* as a second year-round beer in 1996, then later a *leichtes* (light) *weizen*. Kuhn brews a particularly well thought of *weizenbock* for the holiday season.

He begins a tour of the brewery literally at the top, heading up stairs that lead to the mill room. His malt comes from lower Bavaria, his hops from the Hallertau region. (All the ingredients in certified Bavarian beer must come from Bavaria, including the water, which sometimes presents a problem for breweries near the border that draw their water from Austria or the Czech Republic.)

"I know the guys. I know where it comes from and who makes it. I can trust them," Kuhn says. He adjusts his recipes based on the specifications of the malt. "If it is very good, I just do infusion," he says, because that saves energy.

When he says, "I make my beers like my ingredients (dictate)," I think of Luis Barela, a woodcarver in Taos, New Mexico. Barela comes from a family of woodcarvers, and now his sons carve as well. He keeps a large pile of wood in his yard, pieces of cedar he has found in the wild. Barela can look at one and see a finished piece of art, because he will let the shape dictate what he makes.

The analogy is not perfect. Barela carves his nontraditional religious figures based on the grain of the piece of wood he starts with, but Kuhn must adjust *how he brews* because his customer already knows what the final product should taste like. "You cannot always do the same process, because every year the malt is different," he says. "You have to brew good beer out of shitty malt. That's the skill of the brewmaster."

Had Mike Myers played a brewer on "Saturday Night Live," he would have looked and sounded like Kuhn, who sports an earring, wears wire-rim glasses, and pulls his longish hair back in a ponytail. Kuhn speaks excellent English in a precise manner that would perfectly fit the mythical German brewer the late beer writer Michael Jackson created for a story designed to praise the independent nature of Belgian brewers. In Jackson's yarn he asked one German, then another, about making a particular style, always getting an identical answer: "It's the same as Fritz said. That's how you make a Pilsener; that's what we learn in school."

In the discussion about decoction Kuhn has made it obvious he's more independent minded than that, but when talking about open fermentation ("It smoothes out the flavor") and bottle conditioning his beers, he's equally clear about why he continues the practices. "Tradition, of course, but the important thing is to keep the quality," he says.

"We don't have many bad beers in these parts," noted Eric Toft, the Wyoming native who now brews nearby at Private Landbrauerei Schönram.

Thus when Kuhn talks about the year he spent helping to set up the Royal Bavarian Brewery in Moore, Oklahoma, he's bluntly honest in describing the technical shortcomings he saw in the United States in 1994. However, he also remembers liking some beers, including those from Portland Brewing and Tabernash Brewing, two companies eventually absorbed by other breweries. Kuhn and Tabernash brewmaster Eric Warner were already friends, having met when they trained together after Warner completed formal studies at the famous Weihenstephan brewing school near Munich. By 1994 Warner had also written a book called *German Wheat Beers*.

This may be why Kuhn's not sure why I'm here collecting details about how he brews *hefeweizen*. He has a straight-from-the-hip question of his own.

"Eric's book isn't good enough?"

⸺

I had just about the same thought when Ray Daniels, then the publisher at Brewers Publications, suggested I write the book you have in your hands. Granted, *Brewing with Wheat* is about a broader topic, but it was hard not to look over my shoulder, because *German Wheat Beer* is arguably the finest of the books in the Brewers Publications "style" series. While in Bavaria I learned that brewers in the south of Germany use it as a reference, and I only missed by days an opportunity to see Warner make a presentation at Weihenstephan.

Quite simply, he's a brewing expert. I'm a journalist. I collect stories, I ask people what they do and why they do it, I sort through various histories, and I try to make sense of what brewing scientists have to say. Sometimes I draw conclusions, but you are free to look at the same information and connect the dots in some other way.

Which is why one October morning I was watching Bernard Kuhn at work in one of the most hands-on breweries you can imagine, and why five months later I was sitting at a table deep inside the massive Anheuser-Busch Companies complex in St. Louis, Missouri, talking about a relatively new family of wheat beers from Michelob Brewing.

A-B built its pilot brewery in 1981 to mimic the full-sized brew house it hugs, so that activity on each floor mirrors that next door. The company began calling the facility Michelob Brewing in 2008, shortly before Anheuser-Busch became AB InBev, advertising it as "Our Brewmasters' Playground." Although Michelob now offers a widening range of brands, the pilot brewery also functions much as before. It is in part a school where future line supervisors train before they head out across the country, a testing ground for every new batch of malted barley or hops, the place where new recipes are first developed, and the one where they are finalized for each of A-B's breweries across the country.

Thus the idea for *Michelob Dunkel Weisse* originated in Fort Collins, Colorado, as part of a regional program A-B began in 2006. The recipe for the beer first called *Ascent 54* (because Colorado has fifty-four peaks of 14,000 feet or more) was then developed at the pilot brewery and brewed in Fort Collins for draft distribution only in Colorado. When A-B decided to take it national, the brewing process for production in Cartersville, Georgia, as well as Fort Collins was established in St. Louis.

The four beers that Michelob put into the sampler pack in 2009 and offered for sale individually in some markets only begin to illustrate the growing diversity of wheat beers brewed in the United States. The package included a colorful "tasting" sheet, so consumers could pour themselves a sample of each of the beers and compare ingredients, color, body, and bitterness levels, indicating that although it took A-B almost a century and a half to begin brewing with wheat the company sees a future in it now. In fact, as this book was in the final stages of production in the fall of 2009, the brewery rolled out another beer made with wheat, *Bud Light Golden Wheat,* promising to support it with $30 million in advertising in the first year. Unfiltered, and therefore cloudy, the beer is spiced with orange and coriander.

Kristin Saviers, a Michelob brewmaster who since has left the brewing industry, talked about using wheat while we tasted two very different spring seasonals—*Honey Wheat,* filtered crystal clear, orange blossom honey apparent throughout, lightly hopped; and *Hop Hound Amber Wheat,* cloudy, modest hopping (25 IBU) balancing caramel sweetness—along with year-round regulars *Shock Top Belgian White* and *Dunkel Weisse.* First brewed as *Spring Heat Spice Wheat, Shock Top* is labeled as a "Belgian-style wheat ale" but isn't at all traditional. It's spiced with coriander and orange, lemon, and lime peels but contains no unmalted wheat in the grist, nor is it fermented with a yeast sourced from Belgium. "We wanted to get the spiciness from other elements," she said.

Saviers said the Michelob team learned that wheat malt can be added as a nuance to enhance the complexity of the malt character and round out the flavor, or it can be added in healthy amounts as the signature flavor of the beer. She also discovered something else wheat malt brings to a beer: It's not barley. "Barley malt has a strong flavor, a beer flavor some people don't like," she said.

MICHELOB DUNKEL WEISSE
Original Gravity: 1.051 (12.7 °P)
Alcohol by Volume: 5.5%
Apparent Degree of Attenuation: 83%
IBU: 17
Malts: Wheat, pale, chocolate, caramel
Hops: Special Bavarian strain, held at yeast bank in St. Louis
Yeast: Hallertau, Tettnang
Primary Fermentation: Proprietary, fermented slightly cooler than other ales
Secondary Fermentation: Proprietary

Dunkel Weisse marks A-B's third flirtation with a wheat beer taking inspiration from Bavaria. The company briefly tested *Crossroads,* which had the signature banana and clove flavors you expect from the south of Germany, in four markets in 1995. It was the first wheat beer Anheuser-Busch had sold since the Bavarian Brewery (later acquired by Eberhard Anheuser) opened in 1852, and it didn't survive the test. When the Michelob Specialty beers debuted in 1996, the lineup included *Hefeweizen,* styled along the decidedly American lines that Widmer Brothers Brewing (pages 115-122) made popular. *Michelob Hefeweizen* was fermented with the same yeast as *Michelob Pale Ale* and hopped with Cascade and Cluster to the tune of 30 IBU.

That beer lasted longer than *Crossroads,* but was a distant memory in 2006 when Michelob introduced *Bavarian-Style Wheat* in a Specialty Sampler Collection available during the holiday season. When the beer returned in the 2007 pack, the *hefeweizen* appeared less cloudy, even when a bottle was rolled before pouring. Additionally, the level of haze varied from bottle to bottle, although this had no apparent effect on the flavor.

Doug Muhleman—then vice president in charge of brewing operations and technology, since retired—discussed that in an email. "The *hefeweizen* is one of my favorites, and we have struggled to get the yeast to stay in suspension," he wrote. "The strain that we use just loves to floc (flocculate) and settle."

How hard can it be to get all the details right in making a wheat beer? Tough enough to challenge the largest brewing company in the United States, but, as the much cloudier 2009 seasonal release proved, not impossible.

About the Book

Before I even signed the contract to write *Brewing with Wheat* I called Eric Warner. We discussed what he would include were he updating and expanding his original book. He mentioned increasing interest in Belgian white beers, the use of clouding agents such as Tanal A, changes in brewing practices in Germany, particularly at larger breweries, and then threw in the wild card: " . . . knowing what I know, the importance of the integrity of the beer."

Integrity is a little harder to quantify than the temperature range for a ferulic acid rest. The integrity of beer in general would have been a good topic for discussion in the book *Beer and Philosophy*. Although the word "integrity" doesn't come up in Chapter 4 of this book, that's what Rob Tod means when he talks about extending the amount of time a bottle of *Allagash White* retains its original character without diminishing that character at the outset.

Bernard Kuhn doesn't need to worry about that. He can suggest his beer tastes best two weeks after conditioning in the bottle, because he sells almost everything he makes right at the brewery. Larger German breweries don't have that luxury, instead putting a one-year "best by" date on their *weizen* beers and declining to talk about what changed within the brew house to make that possible.

Does that mean they are hiding horrible secrets? I have sat with people who have better palates than mine, tasting *Franziskaner Hefeweissbier* right after being told by the brewmaster that the beer was now made with a single-infusion mash rather than by decoction as in the past, and heard them comment on the ongoing, spicy quality of the beer. They didn't taste an integrity problem.

What seems obvious may not be. When Pierre Celis ran the Celis Brewery in Austin, Texas, the recipe for *Celis White* included six-row barley malt. Any self-respecting homebrewer will tell you why six-row barley is an inferior malt . . . even though it isn't. Celis also pasteurized his beer, which some will argue strips away flavor, even as they enjoy pasteurized wheat beers from Belgium or Germany and explain how *Celis White* helped inspire the return of "traditional" brewing in America.

Brewing practices change over time, generally with the goal of improving what's in the glass, and are more easily understood when breweries open their doors. Visitors to New Glarus Brewing Company in Wisconsin take a self-guided tour, which allows them more freedom to wander than would make many brewers comfortable. "We call ourselves a transparent brewery," brewmaster Dan Carey said. "In the modern world people do not trust corporations. We want people to know that when we say, 'This is how we make the beer,' *this is* how we make the beer."

In the coming chapters we'll see how dozens of breweries make, or in some cases made, wheat beers. Before considering how this book is organized, here are some things to keep in mind:

Wheat is not a style. It's an ingredient that contributes to flavor in a variety of ways. In order to give this book some structure, I'll use generally accepted style guidelines to consider various beers but won't forget either what unites wheat beers or makes them different from others.

What's in a name. In Germany, *weissbier* and *weizen* carry the same meaning, and the terms will be used interchangeably here. The same goes for *hefeweissbier* (or *hefe-weissbier*) and *hefeweizen,* referring to a beer that has yeast (*hefe*). *Hefes* include *dunkelweizen, weizenbock,* and *leichtes weissbier* (or *weizen*). *Kristall weizen* beers, more popular in the north of Germany and Austria, are filtered.

Wheat is not the only ingredient in wheat beers. But you should know it's there. Spaten brews *Franziskaner Hefeweissbier* with 70 percent wheat, more than what's in most wheat beers. That means barley malt still makes up 30 percent of the grist. In Belgian white ales spices change the flavors and aromas. Although wheat, the ingredient, adds other positive characteristics such as better head retention, if you are going to bother brewing a wheat beer you'll probably be happier if a drinker can notice the wheat.

Fermentation. The yeast strains used to ferment many of these beers are not forgiving. They have more in common with strains used with strong Belgian ales than they do with English (and now American) strains. In simple, perhaps oversimplified terms: For Belgian strong ales, the goal is to balance esters and higher alcohols; for *weizen* beers, to find a balance between esters (banana and other fruits) and phenols (clove); and in *wit* beers, to balance yeast-generated spiciness against actual spices without wrecking the beer's delicate simplicity.

Bottle conditioning. Wheat beers are effervescent, so they should be carbonated at higher levels than lagers and many ales. That's not possible with most draft systems and requires a little extra effort when bottle conditioning. As German brewer Josef Schneider says, "It's like sex and Champagne, worth the bother." Strong bottle-conditioned beers make excellent candidates for aging, to see what flavors develop over time. Most wheat beers *do not,* more often losing their delicate character and developing unpleasant flavors.

In Part I of the book we'll consider wheat, the grain, both as an ingredient in baking and in beer before brewers and drinkers identified "wheat beers" as something different. Eventually, styles began to emerge, but wheat beers never quit changing. Some styles died and never returned, while others faded only to return more popular than ever.

Chapter 2 examines why wheat beers look different and why they may taste different. There's a tiny bit of science involved, but if I can understand colloidal haze and 4-vinyl guaiacol (translation: cloudiness and cloves), so can you.

The next four parts are organized in much the same way. Each includes three chapters, beginning with an overview and some history of the styles, then visits to well-known and not so well-known breweries, finally offering a recipe or four contributed by an accomplished brewer.

Part II focuses on the white ales of Belgium, which were brewed for hundreds of years before Pierre Celis picked one recipe and revived Belgian white beer or *witbier*. Brewer/historian Yvan De Baets helps us understand the intricate processes used by breweries around Leuven before the twentieth century. Then we'll step into modern brew houses from Flanders in Belgium to Portland, Maine. Jean-François Gravel of Dieu du Ciel! in Montreal provides the recipe.

In Part III we'll revisit the southern German *hefeweizen* beers featured in *German Wheat Beer*. Weissbierbrauerei Schneider & Sohn, the largest brewery still using all traditional methods, both represents history and employs thoroughly modern practices. In 2009 America's largest ale brewery, Sierra Nevada Brewing, set out to make the most traditional-tasting *hefeweizen* widely distributed in the country and discovered that is not so easy in a brewery built for something else. Homebrewer Bill Aimonetti shares a recipe that has won awards in numerous competitions.

Part IV starts with the story of *Widmer Hefeweizen* and includes many breweries that are American and brew with wheat but don't make beers that fit the standard "American wheat" guidelines. Beers such as *Crack'd Wheat* from New Glarus Brewing and *Gumballhead* from Three Floyds Brewing represent ongoing change, as does Jolly Pumpkin's *Weizen Bam* (a German *hefeweizen* gone "wild" in wooden barrels), one of many likely to further confuse efforts to classify wheat beers. Steven Pauwels of Boulevard Brewing and Todd Ashman of FiftyFifty Brewing then take two very different approaches in their recipes for wheat wine.

Visit Berlin and Leipzig in Part V to learn about Berliner *weisse* and Gose, respectively. Curiously, more brewers in America are taking a shot at making beers that go by those names than anywhere else, including Germany. For recipes, Kristen England starts with his carefully researched, award-winning recipe for Berliner *weisse,* then explains his affection for Gose, Lichtenhainer, and Grätzer (also known as Gridziski).

Part VI wraps things up, with a closer look at "brewing to style," many examples of these beers by the numbers, suggestions for better understanding the various styles, and tips for doing a better job if you judge them.

What's not in the book? For starters, if you have come looking for clone recipes you will be disappointed. You're not going to find a duplicate of *Schneider Aventinus.* I explained in the introduction to *Brew Like a Monk* why I would rather brewers make a beer their own, so I won't repeat that here.

Also, I wouldn't begin to attempt a list of outstanding beers in these various categories, let alone pretend those visited constitute any sort of "best" list. I know that Flying Dog Ales, Victory Brewing, Gordon Biersch Brewing, Stoudt's, and many others make excellent German-style *weizen* beers. I drink *Avery White Rascal, Flying Dog Woody Creek White* and . . . we're just getting started and just in the United States.

Walter König of the Bavarian Brewers Association estimates that about 90 percent of the 628 breweries in Bavaria make at least one wheat beer, some several more. An additional twenty to twenty-five breweries elsewhere in Germany, some of them rather large, also produce wheat beer. That adds up to maybe 580 breweries in Germany and well over 1,000 brands.

You will need more than this book if you want to start brewing wheat beers. Plenty of excellent basic brewing texts, such as John Palmer's *How to Brew,* explain the basics. More technical publications are available should you decide to dive into challenges like culturing yeast strains.

You also won't find information about brewing fruit beers, rye beers, or *lambics,* even though *lambics* are made with wheat. Jeff Sparrow's excellent *Wild Brews* could have been subtitled, "Everything you always wanted to know about *lambic* but were afraid to ask." Randy Mosher's *Radical Brewing* includes the basics about brewing with fruit and a little about rye.

Back to what *is* in the book. Along the way brewers are going to tell us about the challenges of brewing with wheat. Some call it difficult, some easy. Weissbierbrauerei Schneider brewmaster Hans-Peter Drexler makes it almost clear why. "To me it is very hard to do in a traditional way," he said. "Because of the microbiology. You have to look at the details."

On to the details.

PART I:
WHEAT, THE OTHER BREWING GRAIN

chapter one

WHEAT, BEER, AND BREAD

*"For hundreds of years, wages were paid in breads, the average peas-
ant receiving three breads and two jugs of beer a day."*
                                        -Heinrich Jacob, Six Thousand Years of Bread

The Bavarian Brewery and Bakery Museum in Kulmbach in Franconia constitutes
two museums, with separate entrances to brewing history and baking
history, and a visit to one or both establishes the strong and grainy link
between beer and bread. Appropriately, they reside on the grounds of
the former Mönchshof cloister and brewery (and *Mönchshof Schwarz-
bier* is one of several brands made at the nearby Kulmbacher Brewery).

Neither museum limits itself to Bavaria, both focusing on the last
couple hundred years and what the brewing and baking industries were
really like. So while learning that Franconians sometimes blended beer
with soup one hundred years ago makes us smile, pictures of eleven-
year-old children who labored fifteen hours a day, six-and-a-half days
a week illustrate just how hard and sometimes dangerous brewery and
bakery work was. The social history of Franconia makes it clear that
beer and bread were both considered life staples but were also competi-
tors for the same raw ingredients. Additionally, the characteristics that
make wheat particularly well suited for baking bread do not match the
traits that brewers are looking for.

We study history for many reasons. Brewers may look at ancient recipes and brewing practices for inspiration. Examining the past helps us understand change—why some things changed, others didn't, and others may in the future. Geography may also look different through the lens of time. For instance, Belgium wasn't even a separate country when brewers started using unmalted wheat in white beers. Instead of talking about beers that developed in Germania, grab a map and trace a line from the Senne Valley near Brussels to Grodziski in Poland, then draw an oval that also includes the Leuven area in Belgium, Berlin, and Leipzig. Draw another oval or circle that encloses Nürnberg and Munich in Germany. Do you think wheat beers from Hamburg, "the queen of all white beers" in the sixteenth century, would have been more like those in the top oval or the bottom? History doesn't provide a clear answer, and it's an easier question to consider if you discard the notion that all German beers are like the *weizens* of the south, virtually the only variety exported from Germany these days.

In *Six Thousand Years of Bread* Heinrich Jacob writes about how America became Europe's wheat supplier, mostly to bakers, beginning in the nineteenth century. By then the grain shortages that sometimes restricted use of various grains were mostly in the past, although brewers still had to deal with governmental regulations, taxes, and shifting consumer preferences. Bakers faced similar challenges after the victorious French armies convinced neighboring nations, many of them once loyal consumers of rye breads, that a "master race" ate only wheat. Jacob explains that rye was under attack:

"In the Middle Ages Europeans were very fond of the taste of rye. Some of the East Germans had called themselves *Rugii* (rye-eaters)—undoubtedly to distinguish themselves from the ignoble eaters of oats. In Anglo-Saxon England August was called *Rugern*, the month of the rye harvest. As late as 1700 rye formed 40 percent of all English breads; around 1800 the percentage had dropped to 5.

"Where rye bread was firmly established—in large parts of Germany and Russia—it remained. Physicians and farmers insisted that people who for centuries had eaten the dark bread of their fathers, which gave forth a spicy fragrance like the soil itself, could not find the soft white wheat bread filling. They pointed to the physique of the Germans and rye-eating Russians. The wheat-eaters countered with the claim that rye made those who ate it stupid and dull. Wheat-eaters and rye-eaters spoke of one another as do wine drinkers and beer drinkers." [1]

Drinkers had similar debates about beers brewed with wheat and those brewed with barley. An ongoing argument centered on whether wheat or barley made healthier beer. One thirteenth century essayist claimed that beer made with oats and wheat did not cause as much gas as one that also included barley in the recipe. He wrote that beer made from rye or rye bread with mint and wild celery as additives was the best kind of beer.

Among the items on display in Kulmbach is a piece of earthenware discovered at a Celtic burial ground nearby. Scientists found residue of wheat beer that is believed to be almost 3,000 years old in the crock. Of course there's evidence beer existed thousands of years before that, and if emmer, a type of wheat, wasn't included in recipes from the very beginning, it soon became a grain used much like barley, oats, and, later, rye.

Wheat was simply another ingredient in many beers before and during the Middle Ages. Sixteenth century beer writer and expert Heinrich Knaust reported that the widely popular beer from Einbeck, first exported to Hamburg in the eleventh century and by the thirteenth shipped much farther by members of the Hanseatic League, was made with two-thirds barley and one-third wheat. "Of all summer beers, light and hoppy barley beers, the Einbeck beer is the most famed and deserves the preference," he wrote. "Each third grain to this beer is wheat; hence, too, it is of all barley beers the best." [2] Einbeck beer was top fermented "but very different from the top-fermented beers of nowadays," and hopped very strongly. Of course the name "bock" comes from Einbeck, although it evolved into a much different beer when it migrated to Munich.

Governments regulated the amount of wheat that could be included in brewing, sometimes outlawing its use altogether during times of grain shortages. Because of the famine of 1315 London prohibited the malting of wheat to make beer. In contrast, in 1556 Holland's government ordered brewers to water down their beer and use wheat instead of barley,

---

[1] H.E. Jacob, *Six Thousand Years of Bread* (Garden City, N.Y., Doubleday, Doran, and Co., 1944), 290.

[2] John P. Arnold, *Origin and History of Beer and Brewing From Prehistoric Times to the Beginning of Brewing Science and Technology* (Chicago, Alumni Association of the Wahl-Henius Institute of Fermentology, 1911; reprint, BeerBooks.com, 2005), 293.

since the latter would make more nutritious bread. Later maltsters were allowed to use only wheat not fit to eat.

Brewers often changed the grains they used—primarily barley, wheat, oats, and rye—based upon cost and availability. Not all were malted. Many towns set a *pegel* (standard) for beer production, regulating the strength and the composition of beer. From the thirteenth century on the *pegel* for different towns indicates that brewers began to use more barley and less wheat. Certainly, the implementation of the Reinheitsgebot in 1516 further altered the landscape in parts of Germany, eliminating what might be called the casual use of wheat in small percentages. Among other things the "beer purity" law allowed barley as the only grain in beer, ensuring that wheat and rye would be reserved for breadmakers. However, it was not as disruptive as it might appear, because it was valid only in Bavaria until 1906, and Bavaria did not encompass the territory it does now. More important, for hundreds of years royalty granted licenses to brew beer with wheat, until production ceased to be lucrative.

England placed a much more meaningful ban, lasting almost 200 years, on using wheat. Like those on the Continent, British brewers had long used wheat—originally emmer, carried from the Middle East throughout Europe by Celts—as an ingredient. That changed with a prohibition on commercial brewing using anything other than malted barley (which was taxed and an important source of revenue) from 1697 until 1880.

Private households could continue to brew with wheat, and as author Martyn Cornell writes in *Amber, Gold, & Black: The Story of Britain's Beers*, two interesting styles survived until the mid- to late nineteenth century: West Country white ale and mum. Mum likely took its inspiration from a fourteenth or fifteenth century German beer called *mumme* or *mum*, shipped to England from both Brunswick and Lübeck (one of the relics that didn't quite fit into Part V of this book). Mum was the only wheat beer specifically permitted under England's malt-tax laws.

A recipe for mum from John Houghton, a Fellow of the Royal Society, from 1683 looks like one a beer revivalist would want to tackle. Cornell provides the details: "To produce forty-two gallons of mum start with seven bushels of wheat malt, one bushel of oat malt, and one bushel of beans. Once fermentation begins thirteen flavorings are added, including three pounds of the inner rind of a fir tree; one pound each of fir and birch tree tips; three handfuls of 'Carduus Benedictus,' or blessed thistle; two handfuls of 'flowers of *Rosa Solis*' or sundew; the insect-eating bogplant, which has a bitter, caustic taste; elderflower; betony; wild thyme; cardamom; and pennyroyal." [3]

In 1768 *Every Man His Own Brewer* offered a similar recipe, adding, "Our English brewers, instead of the inner rind of fir, use cardamom, ginger, and sassafras; and also add elecampane, madder, and red saunders" (which produces a red color in the presence of alcohol, suggesting English mum was red or pinkish).[4] Just a few years later mum production ended. Today few English breweries make wheat beers, at least in significant volumes, but the Brewers Association in the United States recognizes "English-Style Summer Ale" as a distinct style (examined in Chapter 10).

By the sixteenth century, although barley beers were dominant in Germany, wheat beers began to emerge as something distinct. Knaust described about 150 different beers from Germany in 1573, writing, "The noble Hamburg beer is the queen of all other wheat, or white, beers, just as the Dantzic beer has the precedence and is queen of all the barley, or red, beers." He does not mention what Hamburg beer actually tasted like, but there are hints (such as the popularity of the Broyhan beer it inspired) that northern wheat beer was different from what was being brewed in the south. In the coming years, there would be no doubt.

Cord Broyhan, who had trained in Hamburg, brewed the first Broyhan beer in June 1526 in Hanover, in what was said to be an effort to reproduce Hamburg wheat beer. The beer soared in popularity, was sold widely, and soon brewers in other towns made a Broyhan (or Breyhan or one of many similar spellings), turning it into a "style" that would be available until the beginning of the twentieth century. According to one writer, the more wheat the beer contained, the better it was. However, in *Origin and History of Beer and Brewing*, John Arnold states that the recipe was later modified to make it "mostly" a barley beer. Historian

---

[3] Martyn Cornell, *Amber, Gold, & Black: The Story of Britain's Great Beers* (London: History Press, 2010), 152.

[4] Cornell, 153.

Ron Pattinson has unearthed numerous recipes for Broyhan, some quite different from others, but overall indicating that at one moment in time the "style" might have tasted like a cross between Belgian *wit* and Berliner *weisse*. The range, from all barley to sour wheat, illustrates that just because a beer was brewed in a particular way in 1773 in one town and had "the appearance and bouquet of a young wine, and a sweet tart taste," does not mean it was made the same way in 1573 or 1873.

The predecessor of today's southern German *weizen* likely originated in the fifteenth century in Bohemia, at that time part of the Austrian empire. "*Weissbier*" was brewed for nobility and called "new" beer, while the "brown" or "bitter" beer brewed for the populace was labeled "old" beer. *Weissbier* may have first been brewed in Germany by the Duke Hans VI von Degenberg near the beginning of the sixteenth century, and if not he certainly popularized it.

To the north in Lübeck, already a prosperous brewing center, *Weissbrauer* and *Rothbrauer* ("white" and "red" breweries) began operating in turns in 1547. The brewers (180 houses owned brewing privileges) were divided into quarters, and each quarter would brew and sell its allotted share before the next quarter could brew. In Nürnberg, where various thirteenth and fourteenth century laws required brewers to use only barley, "white beer" arrived in 1541 and "red beer" brewers soon suffered. In *Beer in the Middle Ages and Renaissance* Richard Unger indicates this *weissbier* was in fact a wheat beer. That matters, because well into the nineteenth century in parts of Europe *weissbier* simply meant "white beer," which could be brewed with wheat or with air-dried ("white") barley malt. (This is worth remembering when reading English translations of German texts, because there's always a chance the translator didn't know better, read *weissbier* and wrote "wheat beer.") By 1579 four "red beer" breweries in Nürnberg had gone out of business, six others had given up brewing "red beer," and one-quarter of the forty-two remaining were up for sale. In 1583 the town council decided that twelve "white beer" breweries should be reduced to ten.

East of Nürnberg, in Schwarzach, the Degenberg family established the first recorded *weissbier* brewery around 1500. Until 1602, when the last Duke of Degenberg died, they ran the only brewery the ruling Wittelsbach empire allowed to make wheat beer. When the right to brew reverted to the royal family, Maximilian I recognized the popularity of *weissbier* and began building a ducal monopoly, establishing a network of breweries throughout Bavaria. *Weissbier* sales peaked around 1730 but remained strong for decades before dwindling so low the royal family lost interest. From about 1800 until the latter part of the twentieth century, the style Americans know as *hefeweizen* was a poor cousin to the Berliner *weisse* brewed to the north.

Although wheat beer sales thrived earlier in other northern cities, records indicate significant production in Berlin only began in earnest in the middle of the seventeenth century. Wheat beers had an immediate impact, and in 1680, following protests from *braunbier* brewers and winemakers, lawmakers levied a new tax on *weissbier*. Eventually Berliner *weisse* turned into a distinct "specialty," notably sour, and farther south another sour beer, Gose, became the toast of Leipzig. A certain mystery surrounds these beers and a few others, such as Lichtenhainer and Grätzer (or Grodziski), inspiring recreations from American brewers. The *American Handy Book of Brewing* described Grätzer as "a peculiar German local beer produced from about two-thirds of smoked wheat malt and one-third barley malt. The wheat is steeped for thirty to forty hours; germination is allowed to proceed at rather high temperatures so that the rootlets mat densely. Oakwood is used for fuel in drying the malt, the smoke passing through the malt, giving it a peculiar odor." Brewers strew hops over the grain before sparging, fermented it like a *weiss* beer, and "the taste is said to be deliciously tart and winelike."[5]

In the lowlands that would become Belgium, farmers were brewers and vice versa—they grew wheat and used it, unmalted, in making their beers. By 1420 Duke Jean IV ruled that all the brewers in Brabant were required to include wheat to improve the quality of their beers. Extensive descriptions about what wheat beers in and around Leuven—where three distinct variations of white ales emerged—tasted like and how they were made emerged in the nineteenth century. All were quite lactic, infected with *Lactobacillus* and sometimes *Pediococcus*. They shared certain characteristics with some of the beers of northern Germany such as Berliner *weisse* and Leipziger Gose (descriptions of all include "sour milk-like flavors"). The various white styles disappeared from Belgium

---

[5] Robert Wahl and Max Henius, *American Handy Book of the Brewing, Malting, and Auxiliary Trades* (Chicago: Wahl & Henius, 1901), 821.

■■■■ Ancient Grains of Riedenburg

Many small breweries in the wheat beer-rich region near Regensburg acquire their malt from Malzfabrik Riedenburg in the town of the same name. One, Riedenburger Brauhaus, uses a variety of ancient grains such as emmer, dinkel, and einkorn, all wheatlike and all grown under contract with local farmers.

Riedenburger beers

	Original Gravity SG (Plato)	Alcohol by Volume	Apparent Extract	Color SRM/EBC	Bitterness (IBU)
Dinkel	1.047 (11.6 °P)	4.7%	77%	8 (16)	11
Emmer Bier	1.049 (12.2 °P)	4.9%	76%	17.5 (35)	10
Einkorn	1.049 (12.2 °P)	5%	78%	6 (12)	9

Data courtesy of Derek Walsh and breweries

According to *Theory and Practice of the Preparation of Malt and the Fabrication of Beer*, these grains were most common in the south of Germany and Switzerland in the late nineteenth century and known as "Swabian Wheat."

Riedenburger Brauhaus produces 20,000 hectoliters (17,000 barrels) of organic beer a year, widely distributing a gluten-free beer. Its *Historiches Emmer Bier* contains 50 percent emmer in the grist, as well as einkorn, spelt, barley, and wheat malts. The amber beer pours with a massive head, spicy vanilla notes leaping out of the glass. It tastes somewhat of a *dunkelweiss* with dark fruity notes.

Brewmaster Michael Krieger said his brewers treat those grains much like wheat in the brew house, using a decoction mash and slow lautering, so from mash-in to knockout takes eight to ten hours.

Ancient Grains of Riedenburg

in stages, so that by the time Leuven Wit vanished Hoegaarden White reappeared. The version that Pierre Celis effectively saved has since spread all over the world, although nineteenth century white beer drinkers would hardly recognize any of the modern-day versions.

Belgian brewers around Leuven apparently made trials with malted wheat in the nineteenth century, but the grain remained part of white beer recipes only in unmalted form. However, brewers in the Hainaut region produced a beer called *grisette* with malted wheat. This style disappeared by the 1960s, although some consumers may be confused, because one Belgian brewery uses the name for a beer that has nothing in common with the original style.

Grisette was brewed with more "modern" techniques and compared in quality to the highly regarded Bavarian beers. "*Gris*" is French for "gray," and the beer would have been a color between the white and brown beers. The three main versions were *grisette jeune* (young), brewed all year round; *grisette de garde* or *de saison,* brewed from September to the end of December; and *grisette supérieure* or "double," which was stronger and used only the first two runnings from a mash (the rest reserved for a "*petite bière*"). The *grisette jeune* brewed in summer included more grain, making it stronger at 10.2 to 11 °P, to protect it against infection. *Grisette de saison* started at 1.048 (12 °P) and the double even higher.

The grist included nine parts barley to one part wheat. Wheat germinated only briefly during malting to ensure the retention of starches, kilning at a surprisingly low temperature of 110° F (44° C), intended mostly to dry the grains. Fermentation took place first in a kettle, then in barrels, and the barrels were regularly topped with the mixed beer and yeast recovered from the first stages of fermentation.

More regional beers like *grisette* and Broyhan once existed, but by the time Michael Jackson wrote his first *World Guide to Beer* in 1977 he found four basic wheat styles: Belgian *lambic* and white (or *wit*), *weizenbier,* and Berliner *weisse.* We associate each of them with a rather specific region—although history shows us that these regions aren't necessarily where they first were made—and when Jackson's book appeared most still weren't brewed far from those regions. That certainly has changed. For example, Allagash Brewing in Portland, Maine, makes an outstanding Belgian white beer and Fujikanko Kaihatsu Company in Japan an excellent *weizen.*

Additionally, in the United States an altogether new, and certainly not homogeneous, breed of wheat beers has been born. In traditional brewing countries a few styles thought lost, such as Gose, were resurrected. Sadly, it seems English mum will not be back. Sir Walter Scott provided what would be the final requiem in his 1816 novel *The Antiquary*, describing it as a "species of fat ale, brewed from wheat and bitter herbs, of which the present generation only knows the name by occurrence in revenue acts of Parliament."

chapter two

WHEAT BASICS: WHY IS MY BEER CLOUDY?

"For German brewers the idea of stable haze is a tough one. In school they teach you how to make brilliant beer. Nobody taught you about consistent haze."

-Dan Carey, New Glarus Brewing

When the wind whips across the barley fields of Idaho in late summer, it takes only a little imagination to envision a brewer somewhere hoisting a bag of malted grain and pouring it into his mash tun. But in Kansas, where wheat fills the amber waves of grain, chances are the crop eventually will yield high-arching loaves of bread.

Less than one-tenth of 1 percent of wheat grown in the United States ends up malted for use in beer. Farmers understand that to earn top dollar wheat must be fat in protein, because the higher the protein, the higher the gluten strength, and the higher the gluten strength, the easier it is to produce those billowing loaves of bread. That the proteins and gluten may present problems for a brewer makes no difference.

Those proteins may act as both friend and foe. Wheat malt not only contains more proteins than barley but also more high-molecular-weight proteins. Additionally, glutens compose 80 percent of the proteins (compared to 35 percent in barley). Friendly proteins in suspension contribute to distinctive cloudiness and lingering foam, but longer term, they may turn unfriendly, resulting in flavor stability issues. Additionally, wheat berries lack husks and add to a thicker mash, which can make lautering difficult. That's a production problem rather than a flavor issue but still another concern for brewers.

Wheat presents challenges for a maltster for the same reasons it is harder to manage in a mash tun. Modern technology has made malting wheat easier, but much of what was true in the nineteenth century is true today:

"In some countries wheat is used for the production of local beers, either unmalted as raw fruit or as wheat malt, for instance, in Belgium and in North Germany for the production of *weiss* beer. Wheat malt gives to beer the so-often-desired light color much better than barley malt. But the malting of wheat is a very difficult matter, partly because it is a naked fruit, and partly because in germinating, the cotyledon appears on the same point of grain shortly after the radical has made its appearance. The gaining of wort from wheat (lautering) is difficult on account of the tenacious layer of grains. The wort is frequently cloudy, the beer from wheat is difficult to clarify, and is said not to keep well." [1]

Although British laws prohibited commercial brewers from using wheat between 1697 and 1880, private households could continue to brew with the grain. At times when barley became expensive, brewers sometimes included large percentages, apparently with mixed results. John Levesque, a Sussex brewer and author, wrote: "From many communications the author has had with those who have brewed with wheat malt, either alone, or mixed, [they] complain of a heaviness of flavour, and not altogether so pleasant as the liquor brewed from barley malt." [2]

Not surprisingly, wheat itself affects both how wheat beers look and how they taste. This chapter focuses on how to make beers cloudy and keep them cloudy, and then the first half of the equation for creating the phenolic flavors associated with many wheat beers. The second half of that equation depends on yeast and fermentation, particularly when brewing *weizen* beers, which is discussed in Chapter 8.

---

[1] Julius Thausing, Anton Schwarz, and A.H. Bauer, *Theory and Practice of Preparing Malt and Fabrication of Beer* (Philadelphia: Henry Carey Baird & Co., 1882; reprint, BeerBooks.com, 2007), 198.

[2] John Levesque, *The Art of Brewing and Fermenting* (London: Thomas Hurst, 1836), 20.

■■■ The Vocabulary

Red wheat versus white wheat. The color refers to the seed coat. Some brewers suggest that red wheat contributes a rounder, fuller flavor. Bakers prefer red winter wheat for artisan breads.

Hard wheat versus soft wheat. Hard wheat often has higher gluten content and higher levels of protein. Soft white wheat is used mainly for bakery products other than bread.

Spring wheat versus winter wheat. Winter wheat is planted in the fall, then goes dormant over winter. Spring wheat is planted in the spring and harvested in the fall. Other variables are more important, although winter wheat berries are usually slightly larger, and some bakers call winter wheat "more mellow."

All of the above occur in various combinations, such as "winter hard red."

Unmalted wheat. Also known as raw wheat (or simply wheat), and just what it says. As you will read in Chapter 3, farmer-brewers in Belgium once used a large percentage of unmalted wheat in making nineteenth century white beers, because that was the readily available grain. Many modern-day brewers continue the practice. Homebrewers may purchase something similar in health food stores, although using raw wheat is not quite that simple. For starters, milling takes extra work—it is difficult enough that Brouwerij Van Steenberge in Belgium, which brews *Celis White* under contract, buys milled wheat (flour) otherwise intended for baking.

Many brewers feel raw wheat magnifies the qualities malted wheat adds to their beer, such as a firm body, but it adds no enzymes and can be a nightmare to lauter. That's why many brewers, particularly those limited to an infusion mash, choose to use torrified or flaked wheat instead.

Torrified wheat. Pregelatinized, heat treated to break the cellular structure, allowing for rapid hydration so malt enzymes may attack the starches and protein. May be used in place of raw wheat in Belgian white ales. "It removes the raw flavor," said Bob Hansen, manager of technical services at Briess Malt & Ingredients Company. "To perceive the fullness you need to try it side by side with raw."

Flaked wheat. Briess uses red wheat for its pregelatinized flakes. "They go into solution easier and taste slightly closer to raw wheat," Hansen said. Using too much flaked wheat can lead to lautering issues, but not to the extent that might occur milling raw wheat into flour.

Partly Cloudy to Cloudy

A cloudy presentation broadly unites wheat beers, although obvious exceptions exist. Germany's younger drinkers fueled a resurgence in *weissbier* popularity in part because it looked "natural," containing both "whole grains" and yeast in suspension. This might have been only marketing, but women's magazines touted the benefits of *weissbier* for the skin, and other publications listed the wide variety of vitamins in yeast. (They probably should have mentioned that brewer's yeast contains more uric acid than most other food products [more than double baker's yeast, which itself is higher than most], and that increased levels of uric acid in the blood may lead to gout.)

Cloudiness also helped American beers such as *Widmer Hefeweizen* and *Boulevard Unfiltered Wheat* establish themselves as something different. "People drink with their eyes," said New Glarus Brewing's Dan Carey.

Andreas Richter, quality manager at Weyermann Malting Company in Germany, makes it clear that maintaining permanent haze (as opposed to chill haze—which occurs because proteins remaining in lightly filtered or unfiltered beers precipitate when chilled and disappear as the beer warms) is complex. "It depends on both the yeast strain and the wheat variety," he said. "The big part is not yeast but proteins. Especially the stable cloudiness." Yes and no. New studies indicate just how complicated long-term haze stability can be.

Several academic papers from Belgium indicate larger quantities of wheat in the grist may reduce haze stability. You might want to read that again. One study included unmalted wheat, the other malted wheat. In both cases researchers found that haze intensity increased at wheat levels of 15 to 20 percent, then began to decrease with additional wheat additions, so that at 40 percent beer contained almost no permanent haze after just three weeks. The particles obey Stokes' Law: "Wheat gluten proteins were found to be haze active in that they interact with polyphenols and protein-polyphenol complexes. At low gluten levels, a haze is formed, although at higher gluten levels, these insoluble complexes are too large to stay in suspension and precipitate." [3] Basically, small particles stay in suspension, while larger ones drop out.

No doubt there are lessons to be learned from the research, including the relationship between polyphenols and yeast in suspension, but for hundreds of years brewers in Europe have used up to 70 percent wheat, and their beers have been quite cloudy. Keys are a protein rest at 122° F (50° C) during mashing and using a nonflocculating yeast. In the coming chapters brewers will provide more detail.

Twenty-First Century Solutions

Several German breweries that put a one-year best-by date on their beers package *hefeweissbiers* without yeast, carbonating them in tanks and using flash pasteurization to assure proteins remain in suspension. One theory is that this denatures the smaller proteins, assuring they will not clump together and fall out of suspension (and that they may be more easily roused). By removing the yeast, the breweries assure it will not drag down proteins as it settles. In fact, breweries use such methods in different combinations—for instance, one might centrifuge beer to remove the largest proteins, then flash pasteurize it before bottling with a nonflocculent yeast.

Draft *hefeweissbier* is relatively new in Germany—Weissbierbraurei Schneider, for example, did not start kegging beer until 1993. Schneider ships its kegs upside down so that yeast will be stirred just before a keg is tapped. Additionally, many breweries on either side of the Atlantic train their customers to rouse yeast before pouring.

American pub brewers, knowing their wheat beers will be poured from serving tanks holding seven barrels or more, don't have that luxury. Some, as well as packaging microbreweries, have turned to additives to provide stable turbidity. One, Tanal A, is extracted from Chinese gallnuts, which contain the highest naturally occurring level of tannin. "The structure is similar to a polyphenol," explained Jess Caudill of Wyeast Laboratories, which sells the additive. "It acts like chill haze and eventually will settle out." Developed in Belgium as a fining agent for the wine industry, it crossed over into the beer world. Tanal A is used to maintain cloudiness, Tanal B to remove haze. "It's growing in popularity," Caudill said. "We have quite a few customers who use it all the time, but they don't market that fact."

---

[3] Filip Delvaux, Floris J. Combes, and Freddy Delvaux, "The Effect of Wheat Malting on Colloidal Haze of White Beers," *Master Brewers Association of America Technical Quarterly* 41, no. 1 (2004), 27.

Derek Osborne, director of brewery research and development for BJ's Restaurants, enthusiastically endorses Tanal A. He uses it in both *wit* beers and *weizen* beers at BJ's Chandler, Arizona, brewery and has won medals at the Great American Beer Festival and World Beer Cup with them. "We figured we are the R&D brewery, so we might as well give it a try," he said. Now other members of the chain follow the same recipe. "A little goes a long way, and the lower amount of yeast in your beer, the better," Osborne said.

Tanal A must be hydrated in de-aerated water or carbonated beer, then blended with a batch post-fermentation at a rate of about 4.5 grams per 31-gallon barrel.

Brewers Supply Group sells the second alternative, called Biocloud. A yeast-derived cloud system extracted from primary-grown *Saccharomyces cerevisia* cells, Biocloud is added post-filtration at between 40 and 100 grams per hectoliter (roughly 45 to 120 grams per barrel). "It disperses really well," said John Guzman of Brewers Supply. "There are no problems with stratification."

You Say 4-Vinyl Guaiacol, I Say Clove

What does wheat taste like? I'm not sure I could tell you, and over the course of a year I didn't talk to a brewer who came up with a definitive answer. Bob Hansen of Briess Malt did as good a job as any, saying, "Wheaty, earthy. It is different, but you'd be surprised how nondifferent it is. You can use wheat to make a Pilsener."

Steven Pauwels at Boulevard Brewing in Kansas City, Missouri, likes the character unmalted wheat adds. "It brings a crispness that's hard to describe. A little drier, makes a beer more drinkable," he said.

Darron Welch, brewmaster at Pelican Pub & Brewery in Pacific City, Oregon, views wheat as a facilitator. "I think it has a bready flavor," he said. "Because it is foam positive, it changes how yeast brings other flavors into play."

German brewing literature indicates that wheat *by itself* has little influence on esters and other fermentation by-products—but yeast quickly changes that. Although brewers long ago mastered delivering the clove-like aroma and flavors that help define German *weizen* beers, and to a lesser extent Belgian whites, not until the 1970s did they discover that *weizen* and other "Phenolic Off-Flavor" (POF+) yeasts convert ferulic acid to 4-vinyl guaiacol, the phenol responsible for that character. These include *weizen* and *wit* yeasts in varying degrees, but also yeast used to ferment Belgian strong ales and even English ales. In fact, Guinness & Company did some of the first research into ferulic acid, in their case so they could *avoid* producing ferulic acid during the mashing process, because it would interact with yeast during fermentation to create unwanted phenolic flavors.

Barley and oats contain significant amounts in the subaleurone layer. Wheat has it primarily in the aleurone, which matters mostly because recent studies indicate that although wheat contains much higher levels of ferulic acid, it is released from its bonds with barley malt more easily than from wheat. It is freed by water extraction and enzymatic activity and maximized at temperatures between 104 and 109° F (40 to 43° C) with a pH of 5.8. Other studies suggest a temperature of 113° F (45° C) and a pH of 5.7. The latest indicates that mashing-in at 131° F (55° C) rather than 113° F (45° C) results in a 30 percent lower 4-vinyl guaiacol content in the beer. [4] Like recent studies centered on permanent haze, this one concludes that malted barley selection can be as significant a variable, in this case in flavor and aroma formation.

The takeaway: Depending on brew house limitations, there are numerous way to adjust the clove character in a wheat beer after choosing a POF+ yeast. It could be as simple as changing the balance of barley and wheat malts or using different varieties but could also include altering the length of the ferulic acid rest.

The German View

On an average day, if twelve trucks arrive at Weyermann Malting in Bamberg, Germany, one will be sent home because the grains aren't up to Weyermann's standards. The malting company works with 500 farmers, deciding in advance what varieties of barley will be grown for malting, and about 8 percent will fail one of many tests, such as "ability to germinate" or "level of proteins."

"In former times we had to use bakery varieties for beer," said plant manager Juergen Buhrmann. "Now there are specially developed malts,

[4] N. Vanbeneden, T.V. Roey, F. Willems, F. Delvaux, and F.R. Delvaux, "Release of Phenolic Flavour Precursors During Wort Production: Influence of Process Parameters and Grist Composition on Ferulic Acid Release During Brewing," *Food Chemistry 111*, no. 1 (2008), 91.

but a few breweries still want to use the baking varieties." In December 2008 Weyermann malted five varieties of wheat, and Richter said the company was working with corporate wheat growers to develop more. "There's a huge importance that we as maltsters pick out the best varieties for mashing and brewing," he said.

Weyermann Red Brick Wheat Beer

Weyermann describes this beer as full bodied and fruity. Aromas includes banana, peach, and clove that combine with distinct caramel malt flavor.

Original Gravity: 1.050 (12.5 °P)
Final Gravity: 1.014 (3.6 °P)
Hops: 15 BU (Perle)
Alcohol by Volume: 4.7%

Grain Bill:
Weyermann Vienna 33%
Weyermann pale wheat malt 25%
Weyermann dark wheat malt 25%
Weyermann Caraamber 13%
Weyermann Carared 4%

Mashing:
Mash-in at 99° F (37° C), 20 minutes at 122° F (50° C), 45 minutes at 145° F (63° C), 20 minutes at 162° F (72 °C), mash-out at 171° F (77° C)
Yeast: Fermentis Safbrew WB-06

In 2006 Buhrmann and Richter, along with Dr. Jens Voigt, who teaches at the Weihenstephan brewing school, tested three new wheat varieties. They presented the results at World Grains Summit 2006. Even though two of the three had relatively high levels of protein (13.5 percent each), all produced beers that a tasting panel rated almost exactly the same.

"The sensoric analysis gave similarly high results," their paper concluded. "This means that all brands (varieties) are equally suitable for the production of wheat beers from a sensoric point of view. No off-flavors occurred. All varieties offer the possibility of specific characters of wheat beers by using alternative hopping and fermentation schemes."

The conclusion illustrates Weyermann's philosophy that a maltster delivers wheat "that works" regardless of specific variety. That's somewhat different from malted barley. In 2005 Weyermann brewed four Pilseners on its pilot system, each with malt produced from a different barley, and in a blind tasting an international taste panel had no trouble telling them apart. As a result, several American breweries began ordering Pilsener malt made from a specific barley. Brewers don't make similar requests when ordering wheat. "We know the variety but don't publish it. It's not fixed," Richter said. "U.S. brewers need a product that will work in their brew house systems, and they are asking for higher protein in wheat than barley."

Wheat accounts for 10 percent of production at Weyermann.

The other part of the equation at Weyermann includes the actual malting, a process it holds mostly proprietary. "Each year it's individual. Designed for every crop," Richter said. Buhrmann added, "If necessary you will have different germination times, change kilning so the flavors are homogeneous."

Weyermann test drives each variety in its research brewery, varying methods—using infusion and decoction mashes, in both open and closed fermentation vessels, for instance. "With wheat malt we are looking for a good base, so you can use all the other regimens you want," Richter said.

"In Germany we have breweries that only do decoction for *pils* but will do (step) infusion only for wheat," Buhrmann said. "If you have the philosophy of using decoction, you will hardly go away from it. Infusion, open fermentation, the same."

German brewers understand there's more than one way to brew a wheat beer.

PART II:
THE WHITE BEERS OF BELGIUM

chapter three

IN SEARCH OF THE REAL BELGIAN WHITE ALE

"This yeast is very white, and retains something of the sour taste which is peculiar to all the beer that is brewed at Louvain."

-*David Booth*, The Art of Brewing

Belgian beer history literally covers the walls of the Brussels apartment where Yvan De Baets lives, most of it in books containing surprises he can't wait to discover so he can set history straight. When asked a question, he is not content to pass along the first answer he finds. For instance, discussing a text by G. Lacambre published in 1851, he explains the book is "marvelous, rich, extremely well made, probably the best of the time, but it can't be the only source for a serious brewing historian."

His meticulous research provides a look at three different white beers made in the Leuven region as early as the fourteenth century, with details about production in the nineteenth century: Leuven Wit (Blanche de Louvain in French), Peeterman, and Hoegaarden, the latter more rustic and local.

Because the white beer style disappeared before Pierre Celis revived it in the town of Hoegaarden, most drinkers—in Belgium, in America, and around the world—tend to think what he brewed defines the style. History shows otherwise. Before investigating how today's brewers make such beers, let's look at the originals. They were quite popular

The author with Yvan De Baets. (Photo courtesy of Katherine Longley.)

until World War I and often were imitated by brewers from other cities. The beers were refreshing, both brewed and consumed during the summer at a time when summer brewing was an exception. They were made with winter barley (high in protein) and raw wheat, which, considering the season, meant they would have been infected. According to author Adolphe Frentz, that proved an asset because it allowed the white beers to compete against the *bières de garde* and Bavarian lagers not yet mature enough to drink.

In 1948 brewing scientist Jean De Clerck found all three *always* heavily infected with *Lactobacillus* and sometimes with *Pediococcus*. Lactic character set the beers apart. According to him they tasted mild, the Peeterman darker in color than the Blanche, which he called very refreshing. In contrast, Hoegaarden was extremely sour, sometimes described as containing "sour milk-like" flavors. Although production of all three was in decline, they remained important in the regions where they were brewed.

Nineteenth century brewers took great care to make white beers as white as possible, beginning by using "wind malt," which was germinated at a cold temperature and not kilned at all but simply dried by wind. To keep the beers pale brewers also shortened the boil, although they boiled others for immensely long times. Frentz wrote that the short boiling time did not allow the hops to pass along microbiological protection. In fact, worts often did not even reach boiling, and most of the time only a third of the wort would have been boiled with hops. Additionally, brewers used small quantities of hops, commonly old ones. Little wonder that lactic bacteria, characterized as having a "calming" effect on the stomach, developed easily in all Belgian whites.

Raw grains—mostly wheat but also oats and sometimes buckwheat—made up an important part of the grist in probably all Belgian whites. Recall that brewers were also farmers, and using their own *unmalted* grain was cheap and also added a mellowness considered part of the style. For instance, they included oats to avoid fine-milling the other grains, to make mashing easier, to lighten the color, to make the beer smoother, and to create better foam.

"The use of other sources of carbohydrates, less noble, are sometimes reported as well—as rice, corn, potato flour, sugar, and different syrups. That tendency, nowadays seen almost everywhere, to work cheaply, was already denounced in the nineteenth century, and those beers, too strong, lacking finesse, mellowness, and body were vigorously blamed.

– Yvan De Baets

The beers appeared hazy for the usual reasons—colloidal haze because of the high protein of both wheat and winter barley, and microbiological haze because of bacteria—but also for others. Consumers usually drank them while they were still fermenting, so even more yeast was in suspension than one would expect. The yeast was "dusty," providing a proper hazy appearance today's brewers still appreciate. Additionally, potato starch was sometimes added to enhance the haze, which, Flemish scientist Hendrik Verlinden wrote, would not be lasting.

The methods of production were extremely complex. De Baets counted twenty-one operations between mash-in and pitching of yeast in Frentz's description of the "old method" for Blanche de Louvain. De Clerck reported that mashing for Peeterman could take up to seventeen hours. Saccharification was incomplete, and the spent grains were sparged with boiling water. After that, part of the boiled wort was filtered again through spent grains. This obviously allowed tannins from the husks to solubilize, enhancing the beer's refreshing properties.

According to Verlinden the average original gravity was 1.018 to 1.020 (4.6 to 5.1 °P). Only top-fermented yeast was used, completed by a lactic acid wild fermentation. The attenuation was very low, around 50 percent.

Production of wheat beer halted during World War I, with wheat reserved for bread. After the war customers turned to other beers such as lagers or strong bitter ales, and the white beers survived only near their homes.

Many breweries turned to a more "modern" method post-war, consisting mainly of using metal vessels instead of wooden ones, limiting the time in the coolship, and using a second, more efficient, cooling system. The recipes didn't change, but white beers now fermented with yeast cultures, even though records show lactic infection was still present in most breweries. Bigger breweries that could afford to add kettles adopted a novelty introduced by Lacambre, mashing the raw grains in a separate kettle, called *méthode de brassage mixte* (mixed brewing method, much like what's called a "mash mixer" today). Nevertheless, the general methods remained quite rustic, so that processes described in 1829 (and dating back to at least the eighteenth century) prevailed until 1962.

"The Belgian wheat beers are generally associated with two spices: coriander seeds and orange peels (Curaçao). Very little mention of spices is made in the old treatises. It doesn't mean none were used, though, and it seems that coriander, especially, was often used—but not necessarily always. But it probably proves that the quantity used (when it was used) remained certainly discreet, placing all the modern versions in the category of caricatures. . . . According to Augustine, the consumers liked it only if used in very low amount: as low as one to two grams per hectolitre only."

– Yvan De Baets

Bière Blanche de Louvain

Also Known as Leuvens Witbier or Leuvensch Wit
Grains: Malted barley (45 to 55 percent), unmalted wheat (44 to 56 percent), unmalted oats (6 to 12 percent), buckwheat (rarely).

The 'Old Method' (Being Considered Old in 1872)

As Described By Frentz
Malt underwent a long and cold germination on the floor and was

Beaucoup de

Brasseurs faisant la Bouteille

vendent, en dehors de leur propre fabrication, de la

Bière Blanche de Louvain

Ils augmentent ainsi leurs bénéfices sans accroissement de leurs

frais : dépenses de clientèle, camionnage, etc., etc.

LA BIÈRE BLANCHE DE LOUVAIN

la mieux goûtée est celle des

BRASSERIES VAN TILT, SŒURS

Maison fondée en 1745

Conditions spéciales pour Brasseurs-revendeurs

mashed in with its rootlets intact, imparting an herbal, bitter flavor. Twenty-one separate operations started with a cold mash-in and included six different mashes, three vessels, the use of spent grains for filtration and, as typical, a coolship. The hopping rate was low with old, low-alpha hops.

The pitching rate was also low, creating excellent conditions for bacterial growth. Wort was put directly in wooden barrels, where the fermentation took place. Fermentation started rapidly, and the barrels were turned on their sides so they could be topped regularly with beer. Fermentation took four to five days, after which barrels were topped a last time and sent to customers.

This beer was drunk right after its fermentation, never longer than two to three weeks in summer, four to five weeks in winter. Otherwise, it turned harshly sour. It was served very cold, in jugs, and was apparently at its best eight to ten days after fermentation. Its foam was white and abundant.

Lacambre Method

From 1851

Lacambre was a French scientist who lived in Belgium, consulting in the 1830s at the Brasserie La Vignette in Leuven and instituting many technical improvements. His method for making the Blanche, set forward in his landmark brewing treatise, is more in accordance with the modern methods and should give a better yield and a cleaner taste to the beer.

As in the old method malt was also germinated for a long period, but its rootlets were separated before their use.

Barley and wheat were mashed separately (mixed method). Barley was first mashed in at 104° to 113° F (40 to 45° C). Four other mashes were made, the second by adding water of 176° F (80° C) so that the mash settled around 144 to 149° F (62 to 65° C), and the two last ones by adding water of 194° F (90° C), so they reached 162 to 167° F (72 to 75° C) for a dextrin rest. Gelatinized starch was also present, and in 1829 Jean-Baptiste Vrancken reported he found starch in a six-month-old bottle of Louvain.

■■■A Gose Connection?

De Baets suggests a fourth method must be briefly mentioned because it provides a fascinating link to Leipziger Gose. The grist included eight parts of malted winter barley to four of unmalted wheat and three of unmalted oats, all crushed together. It was mashed in at 59° F (15° C), then rested for 45 minutes. Following a coarse filtration the starchy mash was transferred to the first boiling kettle. A low-temperature fire took two hours to raise the temperature in this kettle to boiling. Meanwhile, a second, then a third and fourth mash were completed and sent into a second boiling kettle.

The wort of the first kettle was transferred after boiling to a coolship, where top-quality aromatic hops were added. After cooling, it went to a fermentation vessel and yeast was added.

In the second kettle, one part of finely crushed wheat was added to the wort, and everything was brought to a short boil. The mash was then transferred into the mash tun, on top of the spent grains, resting for one and a half to two hours. The mash was filtered and pumped into the second boiling kettle. Old hops were added (4 kilograms for 30 hectoliters, about 9 pounds for 25.5 barrels), coriander, plus 250 grams of stag's antler shavings and 1 kilogram of kitchen salt. Everything was boiled until the hot break then sent to the coolship, where fresh hops were added. After cooling to 75° F (24° C) this was added to already fermenting wort in the fermentation vessel. This was put in barrels to finish the fermentation.

"The lactic fermentation, plus the use of salt and coriander, will inevitably make you think to the Leipziger Gose, which has the same characteristics," De Baets said. "It's worth a study on the links between those cities that would show a possible influence in their brewing methods."

The wheat was mixed with cold water then heated in a separate kettle, called a "flour kettle," to which the first and the second runnings of the barley mash were added. A long saccharification rest at around 167° F (75° C) followed. After a boil of five or six minutes wort was left in the kettle for 45 to 60 minutes before being transferred into the clarification vessel. Then the runnings of a fifth mash were added to the "spent flour" left in the flour kettle, boiled briefly, and filtered before being pumped into the coolship.

The two first runnings from that kettle were, as in the old method, directly pumped into the coolship without being boiled or hopped.

The third and fourth runnings were transferred into a copper, where they were boiled with hops. The hopping rate was the same as for the old method: 1 kilogram for 6 to 7 hectoliters (one pound for 72 to 83 gallons). The boiling time was quite short for the era, an hour, so the beer remained pale.

It seems that the "Louvain" was often drunk in one of the numerous pubs of the region, accompanied with a sort of schnapps (a local *genever*, probably).

Twentieth Century Method (1900 to 1930s)
Described by G. Vanderstichele (1905) and Hendrik Verlinden (1933)
Grist: 40 percent unmalted wheat, 50 percent malt, 10 percent unmalted oats.

The grist was divided in two parts with a bit of wheat and most of the barley parceled into the mash tun for a low temperature mash. The rest went into the brewing kettle. The mash was then transferred into the kettle to allow saccharification of the entire grist.

One-third was run off, boiled with hops, and transferred to the coolship. The rest was then transferred to the lauter tun and filtered through the spent grains before being added to the coolship. The mixture was transferred to a buffer tank and yeast added. This was put in wooden barrels, and the barrels were turned so the yeast produced by the fermentation could escape through the bung hole. Attenuation was 50 percent, the alcohol content around 2.5 to 3 percent by volume. Residual extract was high, allowing secondary fermentation in the bunged cask, creating a well-carbonated beer quickly ready to serve.

According to Vanderstichele the beers contained 0.35 to 0.4 percent lactic acid.

Peeterman

The name means "Saint Peter's man." Saint Peter (Sint-Pieter) was the official saint of the city of Leuven, Peeterman becoming the nickname of Leuven's inhabitants.

This was produced much as Blanche de Louvain but boiled longer, and lime (calcium hydroxide) was often added to darken its color, which was yellow to light amber. Vanderstichele writes that darker malts were sometimes used. According to Vrancken, the Peeterman had more wheat than the Louvain. One-third of the wort was boiled with hops.

With a higher original gravity it contained more dextrins and tasted a little sweeter, sometimes being described as almost honeylike.

"In the 1980s I had the chance to taste a Peeterman produced by the last brewery who made it, and I remember a lot of body, smoothness, ripe yellow fruits, and warm biscuitlike flavors, underlined by a refreshing, clean, lactic sourness. An excellent beer indeed."

– Yvan De Baets

The mashing methods employed were similar to the ones of the Louvain, but the Peeterman boiled for three to four hours (similar to boiling times of a 1900s *lambic* wort). The boiling was not only long but also very vigorous, so almost no hop aroma would remain. Old hops from Aalst (near Brussels) were used, a bit more than for the Louvain, commonly 260 to 300 grams per hectoliter (11 to 12.5 ounces per barrel) for a third of the mash.

When a Peeterman was brewed, the brewer always made a "small beer," called in French the *"petite bière blanche,"* with the last runnings and the spent hops.

Starting at 1.059 to 1.075 (14.4 to 18 °P) but fermented with a low attenuating yeast, Peeterman was not quite as strong as it might appear and relatively sweet. It had to be drunk three to four weeks after bottling during summer and six weeks to two months in the winter, remaining hazy for a long time.

Bière de Hougaerde (or Hoegaerde)

Also Known As Hoegaardse Bier

Lacambre indicated that in 1851 the grist included 50 to 60 percent wind-malted barley, germinated slowly, 20 percent unmalted wheat, and 10 to 15 percent unmalted oats. Other reports mention malted oats. In 1933 Verlinden reported a grist we are more used to, with a balance between malted barley and wheat: 43 percent unmalted wheat, 44 percent malted barley, 8 percent malted oats, and 4 percent unmalted oats.

It seems it was drunk mostly locally, although Frentz wrote it was "exported" to surrounding villages in the 1870s, and brewed mainly in the summer.

Apparently the "old method" was widely used until World War I and in some cases longer. In 1933 Verlinden criticized it harshly, astonished that brewers would stick to tradition so near the modern brewing center of Leuven. For instance, many of the utensils were made of wood, as were the kettles, the mash tun and the coolship. Buckets were used to transfer wort.

Lacambre Method

1851

Brewers mashed in at cold temperatures in the summer, lukewarm in the winter, using a partial turbid mash to produce the first wort. They conducted the second mash with boiling water and transferred wort into a copper for a short boil. A third mash, with boiling water, rested for 30 to 45 minutes before lautering. The first worts, called *mees* in local Flemish, were filtered through the spent grains. Then the third wort was boiled with old hops (amounts similar to the Peeterman) for one and a half to two hours. All the worts were cooled in the coolship, then transferred in a buffer tank before being put in barrels, without any addition of yeast, to allow a spontaneous fermentation.

Vrancken, who described a closely related method, wrote that when the fermentation started too slowly some brewers immerged baskets on which some "fermentation material," such as dried yeast and bacteria, was present. The fermentation then started almost immediately. Other brewers would add an unboiled portion of wort to hasten the start of the fermentation.

Verlinden Description
1933

The mash began at a low temperature of 59° F (15° C), was raised to 108° F (42° C) for probably about 20 minutes, then to 131° F (55° C) for 45 minutes. Quick rests at 149° F (65° C) and 158 to 160° F (70 to 71° C) followed. The strong worts (first three runnings) were transferred to a copper, where hops—generally, old—were added (again in the amounts of the Peeterman, low alpha, of course) and the wort was held at 163 to 165° F (73 to 74° C) for 45 minutes, then boiled for an hour. The weak worts (fourth through sixth runnings) followed, boiling two hours with the spent hops only. They were then filtered through the spent grains. All the worts were then transferred to the coolship for one night.

Everything went into 40- and 60-liter wooden barrels the next day, and these were put in a warm room to spark a rapid spontaneous fermentation. Sometimes the wort was first transferred into an open fermentation vessel for two days before being put in casks, where the fermentation began in earnest.

Beer was sometimes sent to the customers after two or three days, always within fifteen.

"Old method spontaneous fermentation, as for the lambic. *It makes a quite strong link between those two styles, even if their tastes and shelf lives were totally different. The grist, the hops, and the fermentation were quite similar, and brewed nearby they shared similar microorganisms. The latter more than one can think: not only the lactic acid bacteria are involved, but obviously different types of wild yeast, including some of the POF (Phenolic Off-Flavor) type. Those are also typically encountered in the first stage of the* Saccharomyces cerevisiae *fermentation of* lambic. *Phenolic flavors are indeed typical of the green* lambic.*"*
– Yvan De Baets

Three main factors set "old style" Bière de Hougaerde apart: the type of cereal used (with wheat, as well as wind-dried malt, providing much of the character); spontaneous fermentation in a wooden coolship (rich with wild yeast and bacteria); and natural acidification by wild lactic acid bacteria (apparently starting before the alcoholic fermentation).

The gravity was around 1.032 (8.1 °P). The beer had clean wheat flavors, an acidic "twang," and was described as "refreshing, agreeable, and healthy." It was very digestible with a sort of "wildness." In comparison to the whites of Leuven and the Peeterman, the Hoegaarde was the sourest, palest, and least smooth. As in the Louvain, gelatinized starch was still present in the finished beer. It was served when still fermenting, in stone or earthenware jugs from the barrel, but was also bottled. Its head was abundant. It was a perfect summer beer, and needed to be drunk within eight to ten days.

At its peak in 1758 the town of Hoegaarden supported thirty-eight breweries, but by the 1930s had only four, and none after the Tomsin Brewery closed in 1957. According to Pierre Celis, eight years later, while listening to others lament the loss of the brewery and the white beer style, he started thinking about opening a brewery. His brewing résumé included only a little time he had spent helping Tomsin when he was younger. Now forty years old, he was delivering milk for a living. However, the retired brewing director of a Hoegaarden brewery, Marcel Thomas, provided expert advice, and soon Celis was setting up an experimental brewery in a cowshed across from his house.

For many, right or wrong, Belgian white and *Celis White* would soon be synonymous.

chapter four

SIX DEGREES OF PIERRE CELIS

"In the beginning I sold only to my neighbors, then to the village, then to the next town, and then Holland and France."

-Pierre Celis

On March 13, 1966, Pierre Celis brewed his first official batch of *Oud Hoegaards Bier*. Brouwerij Celis was in business. Celis brewed fourteen times in 1966, producing 350 hectoliters (less than 300 barrels). Just over five feet tall, from the beginning he described himself as a "small brewer," and given that ten years later he and two helpers made a modest 1,500 hectoliters annually, it didn't necessarily look as if he would be anything more than a revivalist hawking an obscure Belgian style.

But Celis is a man of many ideas. In 1978 he changed the name of his brewery to De Kluis, meaning "The Cloister," and created a valuable monastic connection in the mind of consumers (and later a real connection, brewing a beer under contract for the Trappist monastery Saint Benedictusabdij de Acheles Kluis before it installed its own brewery). He brewed a wide range of sometimes inventive beers, and he understood that larger breweries were more efficient. By 1985 his brewery sold 75,000 hectoliters annually (about 64,000 barrels) and employed thirty-eight.

Breweries large and small, across Belgium and north in the Netherlands, began to imitate his white beer. That even included Heineken with *Wieckse Wit*. "Just about every Dutch brewery has some kind of *wit* in their product range," said Derek Walsh, a Netherlands resident who judges and writes about beer. "Most are insipid, sweetish/citrus-fruity-spicy with nowhere near the grownup dryness and herbal notes that Hoegaarden originally had."

A fire gutted De Kluis in 1985, which was disastrous for Celis because he carried little insurance. He sold a majority stake in the company to brewing giant Artois to finance reconstruction, then expansion and growth resumed at an even quicker rate. By the time he retired in 1990, selling his remaining 40 percent to Artois, the brewery now called Hoegaarden produced 300,000 hectoliters (more than a quarter-million barrels) a year and was about to grow far bigger.

Within two years he founded another brewery, this time in Texas, once again calling it Celis Brewery. One day a University of Texas engineering and chemistry student visited the Austin brewery. "It dawned on me that beer could be brewed here, not just in St. Louis," said Kevin Brand. A dozen years after he graduated and moved to the San Francisco Bay area, Brand returned to Austin and started (512) Brewing Company. He had only been open a month or so in 2008 when Christine Celis, who remained in Austin after the Celis Brewery closed in 2000, called to say her father, Pierre, would be visiting from Belgium and wanted to stop by (512).

When he did he drank *(512) Wit*. When Brand learned Celis would be coming he tracked down a distinctive heavy Hoegaarden glass, the heavy "jar" so closely associated with the brewery, so Celis could autograph it for him. Pierre Celis deserves to be introduced as the man who popularized "Belgian white" beer literally around the world, who accelerated American interest in Belgian-inspired beers and encouraged greater creativity with projects like his own cave-aged beer. But just as important, he remained a "small brewer," one who proved to others "that beer could be brewed here."

Where would you start looking for the "real" *Celis White?* In the town of Hoegaarden, where Celis first brewed his *Blanche Bier?* In Webberville, Michigan, because Michigan Brewing Company bought the Celis brand from Miller Brewing and has won several awards with its *Celis White?* In Ertvelde, Belgium, where Brouwerij Van Steenberge brews *Celis White* for sale in the rest of the world? In Watou, where Celis consulted in developing the recipe for *Saint Bernardus Wit?* Or maybe even in Austin, because when Celis visited (512) he couldn't resist talking shop.

In his biography, *My Life,* Celis provides the recipe for the original Hoegaard *Blanche Bier:* "For every brew of 2,500 liters (one thousand bottles) use 625 kilos raw material such as unroasted malt, oat, and wheat. Oat and wheat are then ground and undergo three process-es with boiling spring waters, successively at 45, 55, and 73 degrees. The mixture remains two hours in a boiler. Then 7 kilos Czech hop is added. This wort chills to 17 degrees and ferments in the yeast tub for seven days. Then follows a secondary fermentation for about a month in beer tanks. This beer is not filtered." [1] Does the fact he listed no spices mean he used none, or, as he often did, wanted to maintain a bit of mystery? Talking about the Austin version of *Celis White* in 1996 he said rumors the brewery used a third spice beyond Curaçao and coriander were untrue. His eyes sparkled when he added, "Every brewer keeps his own secret."

After Celis moved to Texas, growing brewing giant Interbrew acquired Artois and the Hoegaarden brewery. Interbrew later merged with Brazilian AmBev to become InBev, which in 2008 forced a partnership with Anheus-er-Busch, the new company being called AB InBev. At the end of 2005 InBev announced that the Hoegaarden brewery would close and production move to Jupille, Belgium, although packaging facilities in Hoegaarden would stay open. A year later there were reports of shortages of *Hoegaarden White.* "The beer they produce there often has to be thrown out because it is not at all fit for consumption. So a lot of the white beer coming from Jupille is being shipped to the Netherlands to be made into pig feed. It really is a crisis," a union official claimed. At the end of 2007 InBev announced plans to upgrade the Hoegaarden facility and stated that it would be the only brewery in Belgium where it brewed white beer.

---

[1] Pierre Celis, *My Life* (Antwerp, Belgium: Media Marketing, 2005), 43. (Temperatures are in Centigrade.)

HOEGAARDEN
Original Gravity: 1.048 (12 °P)
Alcohol by Volume: 4.8%
Apparent Degree of Attenuation: 77%
IBU: 12
Malts: Malted barley, unmalted wheat
Spices: Coriander, orange peel
Hops: Tomahawk, Nugget
Yeast: House
Primary Fermentation: Yeast pitched at 64° F (18° C), rises to 77° F (25° C), 5 days
Secondary Fermentation: 54 to 66° F (12 to 15° C), 2 to 3 weeks
Also Noteworthy: Centrifuged, then pasteurized before bottling

AB InBev brews Hoegaarden beers in Russia as well as Belgium, but most production is at the 1.2 million-hectoliter (about 1 million-barrel) brewery in the middle of the small town, and includes others beyond *Hoegaarden White*. A massive facility for packaging, refermentation, and warehousing sits outside Hoegaarden, while a roundabout with a copper kettle in the middle signifies a brewery must be nearby. It's a big operation, using 16 tons of dried orange zest and 19 to 20 tons of coriander annually.

Hoegaarden White contains 40 percent unmalted wheat and 60 percent malted barley, with the mash gradually heated from 122° F (50° C) to 167° F (75° C). Lautering that used to take four to six hours now lasts little more than two hours. After a one-hour boil brewers cool the wort to 64° F (18° C) and pitch yeast, allowing fermentation to rise to 77° F (25° C) over the course of five days. The beer is centrifuged and pasteurized. Although Belgians who have been drinking the beer regularly for decades insist *Hoegaarden White* has lost its distinctive character, it regularly wins gold at the World Beer Cup.

Brouwerij Van Steenberge employs a similar recipe, but not the same process, to brew *Celis White*. The brewery uses milled white wheat (between 40 and 50 percent of the grist), otherwise intended for baking, along with malted barley. The mash begins at 122° F (50° C) and is gradually heated, but only to 149° F (65° C) for saccharification. Hops are added with 20 minutes left in the boil, coriander and Curaçao at the end.

Jef Versele pours a beer in the Van Steenberge tasting room.

"The most important is the temperature of the yeasting and the period of lagering," said Jef Versele, Van Steenberge sales manager, whose family has operated the brewery for seven generations. Fermentation starts at 60° F (16° C) and won't be allowed to rise above 64° F (18° C). In contrast, strong Belgian ales like Van Steenberge's *Piraat* may ferment as high at 79° F (26° C). Primary usually lasts eight to ten days. "It depends on the vitality of the yeast. From time to time it will be quicker," Versele said. The beer is centrifuged, and conditioning at about 41° F (5° C) takes four weeks. *Celis White* always conditions in the same fermenter, and only the *White* goes in that vessel.

CELIS WHITE (VAN STEENBERGE)
Original Gravity: 1.048 (12 °P)
Alcohol by Volume: 5%
Apparent Degree of Attenuation: 79%
IBU: 12
Malts: Pilsener, unmalted wheat
Spices: Coriander, orange peel
Hops: Saaz
Yeast: From Pierre Celis
Primary Fermentation: Yeast pitched at 61° F (16° C), rises to 61 to 64° F (16 to 18° C), 8 to 10 days
Secondary Fermentation: 41 to 43° F (5° to 6° C), 4 weeks
Also Noteworthy: Bottle conditioned

Celis provided the yeast. "The yeast, the recipe. His old brewmaster from De Kluis and Texas was here for the first fifteen brews," Versele said. The De Smet brewery originally brewed *Celis White*, but when

■■■ Where Have All the Good Whites Gone?

Joris Pattyn, an international beer judge who has co-authored two books about Belgian beer, admits Belgian white beers are not his favorite style, and there seems to be a reason why.

"If anything can be said, it's that it's lost complexity over the years, constantly," he wrote via email. "I remember slightly aged versions from the very first (Celis) brewery, and it had more complexity than those of latter years. When Interbrew took over it was a complete downward slope. If there's anything I really do remember from the earliest version, it is that the orange (peel) character was more outspoken, rather than the coriander flavor.

"There it is, the C-word. I dislike coriander, once it exceeds (taste) threshold. Some American *wits* are just cold soup to me, because of the coriander excesses."

As he wrote in *100 Belgian Beers to Try Before You Die!* he favors the *Saint Bernardus Wit*, because it resembles the earlier beers Celis made at De Kluis.

"I prefer the wheat beers that are more akin to the Peeterman, or Dobbele Witte (Leuven Wit) style, rather than the old Hoegaarde-specific style."

He couldn't think of a Belgian *wit* today that reminds him of those.

Heineken bought the brewery in 1999 Celis went looking for a new partner. "He said, 'I can't accept my beer would be produced by Heineken. If you can work with Pierre Celis, the godfather of white beer, you must,' " Versele said. "I remember my grandfather was against (doing this). To be honest I can't say he wasn't right."

Van Steenberge had never previously brewed a beer intended to look cloudy. "You do everything to avoid cloudiness. Cloudiness to my grandfather stands for infection," Versele said. "It took us a year, a year and a half, to get it right. We had no experience working with a centrifuge. That was the most difficult part to learn, was the cloudiness."

Celis White conditions at 75° F (24° C) for two weeks after bottling. Van Steenberge packages and conditions beer for breweries from all over Belgium in its modern facilities. Air constantly circulates through the floor-heated warm rooms. The brewery doubled its output in recent years to 75,000 hectoliters a year (about 64,000 barrels). "We suffered some quality control problems," Versele admitted. "It is like working on a farm and going from five or eight cows to twenty-five. You must be ready."

At times Versele seems to have one foot planted in the twenty-first century—using the GPS in his car as a radar detector—and the other next to Pierre Celis, "small brewer." The brewery sits on seven acres in a "living zone," surrounded by houses that assure it won't grow much larger, and his daughter goes to school almost next door to the brewery. The premises date to 1641, and the brewery hospitality pub was built as a stable house in 1780.

Walking into the brew house he asks a question about other breweries his guest visited recently. "How many have soul, my friend?" He looks at the shiny equipment, gesturing toward the computer terminals. "The problem is when (brewers) push the buttons because the computer tells them to. You should know why. When they don't know, it makes me mad."

Van Steenberge brewery sells about 6,000 hectoliters (5,100 barrels) of *Celis White* across the thirty-five countries it ships to, primarily to neighboring countries, Russia, and Scandinavia. "I am very happy we had an opportunity to do this," Versele said. "Too many people are telling the story that they have the Pierre Celis recipe, which is not true."

Saint Bernardus acknowledges just that. "Pierre Celis helped fine-tune the beer, he didn't change all that much, but what he did was a huge help for us," said Marco Passarella, Saint Bernardus's marketing manager. "It is a fine example of how little shifts in the volume of ingredients can make a big difference in the end."

Wit is not the best-selling beer for (512), but Brand likes the idea of keeping the Austin link alive. He spices his with coriander and grapefruit peel and made a few process changes after Celis came to visit. "He had some great stories," Brand said. "Mostly he reinforced some ideas, like a simmering boil and careful use of the chillers on the fermentation tanks to preserve the chill haze."

Aus-Tex Printing and Mailing now occupies what was the Celis Brewery. Celis first sold a majority stake in the business to Miller Brewing in 1995 in order to fund expansion, then the rest of the operation to Miller in 2000. The brewing giant closed the brewery the next year. "It's a huge loss to Austin," Chip McElroy, co-owner of Austin's Live Oak Brewing, said at the time. "It's like if you had an internationally recognized symphony and no one came to hear it. Among beer people, the fact that Austin couldn't support Celis is like Kennedy being shot in Dallas."

Celis said that red winter wheat grown nearby and the relatively hard, limestone-influenced water of Austin both suited his *White* well. He originally used pale barley malt imported from Belgium but later used a mixture of two-row and six-row from the United States. From the beginning in Austin he pasteurized the *White* after primary fermentation and a week of lactic fermentation. Michael Jackson described the early versions of *Celis White* as "very similar to the original Belgian product, though perhaps softer, slightly fruitier, and fuller in flavor."

Michigan Brewing acquired the Celis brand from Miller, along with the entire brewery—a 100-barrel copper dome kettle and mash/lauter tun built before World War II but unused for fifty years before Celis bought it, all the packaging equipment, lab equipment, and even the coriander mill. The brew house remains in storage, but Michigan began producing the Celis brands in 2002, distributing *Celis White* on a limited basis but winning a variety of awards.

IT ALL STARTED WITH A WHITE

Rob Tod took a swig from a bottle of *Allagash White*, held it up to catch a bit of light, and grinned. "This beer tastes like it did when we first brewed it," he said. He doesn't mean *exactly* like in June 1995, but while he spends much of his time on the road talking about Allagash Brewing's more exotic beers, he takes particular delight in coming home to a beer that tastes like it did when he left.

"We're growing," he said, looking around his Portland, Maine, brewery. "As a result we can make a beer more consistent.

"We're going to change equipment. Our goal as brewers is to make sure the flavor doesn't change. I can tell you, as the guy who wrote the recipe and who brewed it, the beer is the same."

Some changes involve process. "Our focus has been on maintaining the flavor of the beer," he said. "Six years ago, it might have been precisely like we wanted it after a certain amount of time. Now we have extended that time dramatically."

Some changes merely reflect ongoing adjustments. "I think we last made real changes in 1996. Maybe altered it in a minor way. Cut down on a certain spice, made it with a little less wheat," he said. "But every batch of grain, we do a work-up on, and then need to tweak something. The coriander seeds get smaller, and smaller are more intense, so we need to cut back."

Head brewer Jason Perkins, who has been at Allagash since 1998, oversees three to four brews a day, four days a week, mostly of *Allagash White*, which accounts for almost 80 percent of production. The recipe includes pale two-row malt from Briess, raw white wheat, and malted red wheat that is milled into a holding tank.

The single-infusion mash ranges from 153° to 155° F (67° to 68° C) depending on the quality of the malt. Hops are added 15 and 45 minutes into the 90-minute boil, then in the whirlpool along with a spice bag containing coriander, Curaçao orange peel, and a secret addition. "We experimented with every way you could think of to add the spices," Perkins said.

ALLAGASH WHITE
Original Gravity: 1.048 (12 °P)
Alcohol by Volume: 5%
Apparent Degree of Attenuation: 82%
IBU: 21
Malts: Pale, unmalted white wheat, malted red wheat
Spices: Coriander, orange peel
Hops: Perle, Tettnang, Saaz
Yeast: House yeast
Primary Fermentation: Yeast pitched at 65° F (18° C), finishes at 68° F (20° C), 7 days
Secondary Fermentation: Begins at 60° F (15.5° C) and drops to 50° F (10° C), 4 to 7 days
Also Noteworthy: Bottle conditioned

Fermentation begins at 65° F (18° C) with a house strain used primarily for the *White,* and the wort is aerated with a stone. Allagash banks the yeast and grows up a fresh batch every three or four months. Primary fermentation lasts seven days but is near terminal in three. Because the yeast count will be around 25 million cells per milliliter after secondary and Allagash bottles with two million, brewers centrifuge the beer, holding the temperature at 50° F (10° C) so it retains its chill haze.

The *White* spends a short time carbonating in a packaging tank and contains about 1.8 volumes of carbon dioxide before bottling, 2.5 by the time it heads to market. "This is a very delicate beer. Oxygen is the enemy," Perkins said. "To get the stability we want we've sacrificed 100 percent bottle conditioning (starting flat)." The *White* conditions at 70° F (21° C) in the four-packs that it will be shipped in, stacked on a pallet with an open column in the middle so the temperature is uniform.

Allagash has a separate barrel room held at 60° F (15° C) for numerous special projects. In 2007 Tod commissioned a small freestanding building that holds a traditional coolship found primarily in Belgian *lambic* breweries. Spontaneously fermented beers—wheat based, in fact—reside in different-sized barrels, but that's another book.

"I didn't set out to make a white the flagship. It just happened to be the first beer we brewed," Tod said. He was working at Otter Creek Brewing Company in Vermont in 1994 when he sampled *Celis White* for the first time. "People were traveling, and they'd bring back beer. Every few weeks we'd have a tasting," he said. Tod quit his job at Otter Creek on June 30, 1994, and The Great Lost Bear in Portland tapped the first keg of *Allagash White* one year to the day later. By then he had brewed eight homebrew batches of *White* and two 15-barrel test batches.

"For the first eight years people weren't interest in Belgian beers," he said. "People would ask us, 'Why don't you make the *White* more accessible?' Get rid of the classic wheat character, take out some spices."

Tod spends much of his time traveling, introducing consumers to what to many remains an odd-tasting beer. When he's back there's always something to do in the office, but he can't stay out of the brewery. "I like to walk through here. I'm not stirring the mash anymore," he said, leaning over the tun and smelling one in progress. "But I'm pouring off the sample valve (on the fermenter). I'm walking by the bottling line to see how it runs. I'm in tune with what is happening here. It's so important for me to be in touch."

Last time work needed to be done on the brewing kettle he did the welding himself. "Whenever you make any changes in brewing the beer you are going to change the beer," he said.

Had he admitted that ten years ago, it would have been because he had heard so many other people say the same thing. "Now I believe it," he said. "At some point we are going to outgrow this system, but we're going to make the same beer."

The Best-Selling American Wheat Beer Ever

Keith Villa. (Photo courtesy of MillerCoors.)

Keith Villa was born just down the road from the massive Coors brewery in Golden, Colorado. He went to high school nearby and to college in Boulder. He had only briefly been working for Coors and had never been east of Nebraska when the company offered to pay his way to study for a doctorate at the University of Brussels.

He eventually earned a Ph.D. with high honors in brewing biochemistry but learned about much more than beer itself during four years in Brussels. "If you were to taste all the white beers in Belgium and then you talk to each brewer and tell him how this one tasted different than that one," Villa said, pursing his lips and casting an eye to the ceiling as he prepared to make his point, "the brewers you talk to, they will tell you *they* have the authentic taste. That's the way brewers are. They are very proud of what they make. They will claim they make the true taste."

He leaned forward. "Back to our style. I would say it is made in the Belgian style."

This was his long answer to a question about if *Blue Moon Belgian White* might better be classified as a Belgian-style *wit* or simply an

---

[2] Since the introduction of *Blue Moon* Coors has merged with Molson in Canada to form Molson Coors internationally. Molson Coors later began a partnership with Miller Brewing in the United States known as Miller Coors.

American wheat beer, albeit one that doesn't match any current style guidelines. The beer Villa created in 1995 turned into the best-selling wheat beer in the United States, though not exactly the best loved. Some people don't care for the beer itself, but more dislike Coors [2] or that the company did its best to hide the fact it owns the Blue Moon brand.

Villa is fond of pointing out, fairly, the beer wasn't the product of a marketing group that decided a cloudy "Belgian" beer would turn out to be hip. It survived because people like it. Like many bricks-and-mortar startups in 1995 *Blue Moon* began without an advertising budget and little love from distributors.

Back from Belgium in 1992 Villa first took charge of new product development. He brewed energy beers and health beers, beers with fruit, beers based on classic styles, and even a peanut butter beer. In 1994 he and Jim Sabia, who worked in the marketing department, were given the task of launching a brand on a shoestring. They had no marketing budget, no distribution deal and, in fact, no place to brew their beer. Villa quickly decided he wanted "Belgian to be our style."

"To me the standard white style didn't have that nice, smooth flavor the American palate would be looking for," he said. He added oats to the mix, hardly rare historically but uncommon in the mid-'90s, and instead of Curaçao he decided to use Valencia and navel orange peels. "Really refreshing, marmalade with vanilla notes," he said.

In 1995 he brewed a batch at the SandLot Brewery at Coors Field, a brewpub Coors owns within the Denver baseball stadium, and called it *Bellyslide Belgian White*. It turned out to be the best-selling beer of the summer. "We knew that would be our lead beer, but we still didn't have a name for the company," Villa said. He continued to write more recipes and brew test batches. "We had an administrative assistant who tasted the Abbey Ale. She said, 'You are making great beer. You have this unique opportunity. This comes around once in a blue moon,' " Villa recalled. As a reward for coming up with the brewery name they had long been struggling to find, they gave her a couple of T-shirts.

Now they needed a place to make the beer. "We were told we wouldn't be making it in Golden," he said, where Coors operates the largest single brewing facility in the world. They struck a deal with Matt

Brewing in New York, which brewed beer under contract for several microbreweries, including the Brooklyn Brewery. Villa would fly back and forth between Golden and Utica, New York, also overseeing brewing at SandLot.

Sales grew, but very slowly. "We didn't really fit into the Coors distribution system until about five years ago," Villa said. Sometimes they would have to wait in line at Matt. "They'd tell us they were brewing Rhino Chasers or they were brewing New Amsterdam," he said, naming contract brands once well known, now forgotten. "They'd get back to us in a month."

Blue Moon production moved to Hudepohl-Schoenling in Cincinnati, then to the Coors brewery in Memphis when Boston Beer bought the Hudepohl-Schoenling plant. Production moved twice more, first to the Molson brewery in Montreal when Molson and Coors merged. It landed at a Miller facility in Eden, North Carolina, when Coors and Miller formed a U.S. partnership.

To make the beers brewed in Denver in North Carolina became the new challenge, and not only because Eden is gigantic and SandLot has a 10-barrel system. Water boils at a lower temperature in Denver because of the elevation, reducing hop utilization. The fermentation vessels are different shapes. "On a good day, if everything is going right and both breweries make their best beers, they'll be the same. SandLot sometimes has a little too much clove (character), sometimes a bit too much spice," Villa said, talking about flavor impressions rather than quantity of ingredients. "Eden is not as artisanal as SandLot. They are a production brewery. They make the beer the same time after time. That's what they do."

"The tough part was getting people to try a cloudy beer," Villa said. He sent out a memo suggesting accounts serve it with an orange. Problem was that bars had only lemons and limes, often to put in the neck of a Corona beer. "Nobody had oranges back then," Villa said. "We'd show up at accounts with a bag of oranges and tell them how to do it. Pretty soon people were calling us asking, 'Where's my bag of oranges?' "

Blue Moon is brewed with malted wheat rather than unmalted, goes through a step-infusion mash, and ferments with the same yeast that SandLot uses for its English ales. The step-infusion mash, protein and fiber from the oats, plus the yeast all contribute to *Blue Moon's* signature cloudiness. "But the yeast will settle out. It's good for six months when it is kept cold," Villa said. "The first thing to go is the nice spice character."

Once it leaves the brewery, the size of the plant where *Blue Moon White* is brewed does not matter. It's just another white beer trying to stay white.

Treating the Spices Right

Brouwerij Bavik takes a different approach to adding spices to *Wittekerke,* its *wit* beer. Instead of following the oft-repeated advice from Pierre Celis to make the additions very late, lest the aroma go up the chimney, its brewers add coriander and orange peel at the beginning of the boil. "We used to do it with fifteen minutes left, but with the microorganisms (on the spices) the danger of infection is too high," said Yves Benoit, who is in charge of quality control. To compensate for what might be lost, Bavik uses larger quantities of coriander and orange.

"We experimented with powder, with liquid form, but dry peels are the best. We mill them ourselves," he said. It's the same with coriander. "When you buy it milled, you lose too much flavor."

Bavik, sometimes referred to as the De Brabandere brewery, is a family-run operation located not far from the city of Kortrijk, and it sells half its production to 800 nearby pubs and restaurants in Flanders. *Bavik Pils* and *Wittekerke* are the best-selling beers, but Americans know the brewery primarily for *Wittekerke* (available in cans in the United States) and *Petrus.*

The brewery, like many others, began making *wit* in the 1990s. The first version, called *Bavik Witbier,* was brewed with oats as well as Pilsener malt and unmalted barley. Benoit said the oats were dropped before the brewery changed the name to *Wittekerke* (after a popular television soap opera). "After doing a lot of tests we found out that oats didn't have a real positive function in the production process and in the final beer," he said.

Wittekerke presented challenges in lautering during a step-infusion mash—122/145/167° F (45/63/72° C)—until a multispeed motor was installed. The *wit* boils for only 45 minutes, to keep the color lighter, with most of the Saaz hops added at the beginning and a small portion at the end. "We want it to be rich in beer aromas, coriander, and orange, and we want flowers," Benoit said. "My boss is addicted to Saaz."

The brewery produces four to eight 150-hectoliter batches a day, more in the summer, racking them into fermenters of between 600 and 1,000 hectoliters (500 to 800 barrels). Brewers pitch yeast with 10 million cells per milliliter, and fermentation begins at 64 to 68° F (18 to 20° C), rising to 77 or 79° F (25 to 26° C) in three to four days. The beer is cooled first to 64° F (18° C) for one day and to 54° F (12° C) for at least a week.

WITTEKERKE
Original Gravity: 1.046 (11.5 °P)
Alcohol by Volume: 4.7%
Apparent Degree of Attenuation: 76%
IBU: 11
Malts: Pilsener, unmalted wheat
Spices: Coriander, orange peel
Hops: Saaz
Yeast: House
Primary Fermentation: Yeast pitched at 64 to 68° F (18 to 20° C), rises to 77 to 79° F (25 to 26° C), 3 days
Secondary Fermentation: 54° F (12° C), at least 7 days
Also Noteworthy: Centrifuged and pasteurized before bottling

Bavik uses the same yeast for all its top-fermenting beers, including *Wittekerke* and the *Petrus* family. Benoit started working at the brewery to implement the yeast program. He keeps each of the brewery's three strains in a refrigerator at home, his boss does likewise, and they are also stored at a university. "Sometimes we'll use them thirty, forty, fifty generations. No problem," Benoit said. When he started there a strain might have been repitched for 170 generations.

A first fermentation is treated differently, starting with a 1.040 (10 °P) table beer. "You should let the yeast know what it is to ferment. It is actually a living thing," Benoit explained.

Most of the *wit* lagers a week or more in 200- or 400-hectoliter horizontal tanks (170 to 340 barrels), but when the brewery is busy in summer some will condition in 600- and 800-hectoliter cylindro-conical tanks. A taste panel can't tell the difference, although the pH measures lower in the 800-hectoliter tank because more carbon dioxide remains in the beer.

Bavik centrifuges but does not filter *Wittekerke* before pasteurizing. "Many people do not understand Belgian *wit* is cloudy from the wheat (protein)," Benoit said. "Not all people all over the world know cloudy is from the wheat. Most people know beers can be cloudy from yeast, bottle conditioning."

Bavik experimented with bottle conditioning. "My colleagues saw that a beer with so much spicing, it's so spicy you can't smell the flavor of the secondary yeast," he said. Kegs contain 2.4 to 2.5 volumes of CO_2, as high as most draft installations can handle, and bottles 3 to 3.1 volumes.

Benoit said that his lab has examined bottles from *wit* producers throughout Belgium and "there are no living cells in any of them."

The brewery began making *Wittekerke Rose* in 2005, adding 10 percent raspberry juice between centrifuging and pasteurizing, compared to 20 to 30 percent juice in several other similar brands on the market. Bavik also includes a tiny measure of sour beer, really only enough to add a bit of tart texture, taken from 220-hectoliter tuns used to make *Petrus Oud Bruin* and now *Petrus Aged Pale*. *Oud Bruin* is a blend of 70 percent dark brown and 30 percent aged pale in wood vessels. The brewery never sold the *Aged Pale* separately until Michael Jackson talked management into bottling a batch for a U.S. beer club bearing his name. It's now a regular offering.

Benoit delights in telling a story about when Jackson would visit the brewery and sit at a desk taking notes. He would ask Benoit to bring him "a bucket" of pale directly out of the wood. The brewery recently added six new 220-hectoliter, French oak standup tuns to go with nine 220-hectoliter wooden horizontal tanks already in place.

Bavik isn't interested in extracting tannin flavors from the wood but is looking for homes for six souring microorganisms Benoit has isolated. "The first fruit beer I had as a student was *gueuze* with real fruit juice," Benoit said. "Now they are adding sugar, sugar, sugar. They are adding more stuff to get it sweeter."

Standing at his desk in the lab he resumed talking about quality control and process. "This is a very easy beer to make. Foam is very good for wheat beers," he said. "The only thing hard is the spices. Every new harvest for spices can be different."

Acting Green and Looking White

Those working on developing a recipe for *Mothership Wit* took what's an unusual approach for New Belgium Brewing, known better for its green practices than adhering to styles. They started by looking at Belgian-style white and *wit* beers on the market, particularly from Belgium. "A lot of our recipes are off the cuff," said assistant brewmaster Grady Hull. "In this case we were going for a style."

They obviously came close, because the beer won a gold medal at the 2008 Great American Beer Festival. The final recipe draws upon tradition, including oats, but also augments the usual coriander and orange peel with lemon peel. The brewers have a long history with coriander and orange peel, since those are part of *Sunshine Wheat,* one of New Belgium's first beers. "Obviously not the same yeast, but we knew some of what we wanted in spices."

MOTHERSHIP WIT

Original Gravity: 1.051 (12.6 °P)
Alcohol by Volume: 4.8%
Apparent Degree of Attenuation: 73%
IBU: 12
Malts: Pale, oats, unmalted wheat (all organic)
Spices: Coriander, orange peel, lemon
Hops: Hallertau
Yeast: *Wit* yeast
Primary Fermentation: Yeast pitched at 60° F (15.5° C), rises to 75° F (24° C), 4 to 5 days
Secondary Fermentation: 30° F (-1° C), duration depends on clarity
Also Noteworthy: Flash pasteurized before bottling

The key was finding a *wit* yeast. "We tried a variety of yeast strains and spices. We didn't want the spices competing with the yeast," Hull said. "Once we found one we added the lemon peel. We also brought up the coriander." Coriander adds a flavor he calls "fruit loops," and he thinks it plays well off a bit of banana (isoamyl acetate) from the yeast.

Mothership Wit merged two projects in 2005, one to come up with a recipe for *wit,* the other to develop New Belgium's first organic beer. "I was kind of surprised how easy the organic certification was," Hull said. He had no trouble sourcing organic ingredients, including unmalted soft white wheat grown in Colorado.

Keeping the *wit* cloudy proved more of a challenge. New Belgium

◼◼◼ Experimenting With Ancient Methods

Early in 2008 Jean Van Roy of Brasserie Cantillon asked Yvan De Baets to create an old-fashioned white that they would brew at the famous *lambic* brewery in Brussels. "The challenge was quite big: We were currently not in position to sell a 'real' old school white," De Baets wrote. "The shelf life of those sour beers was between eight days and two months at the best. Belgium is no real market for that kind of beer anymore." They decided to use a recipe where most of the methods would be ancient, but the goal was to make a beer that keeps longer in the bottle. He explained the process in detail:

"The big issue was the action of the lactic acid bacteria, which we had to keep at a low level. First of all, as we were brewing in a *lambic* brewery, it was out of the question to let anything spontaneous happen. We would have got a *lambic* for sure. Therefore, we left the wort in the coolship until it cooled to 55° C (131° F), then transferred it to a disinfected stainless steel fermentation tank to cool down to 25° C (77° F). So, we had to add cultured bacteria. They like a lot of simple sugars like glucose. If I would have added them with or before the yeast, they would probably have made the beer turn too sour. I decided then to add them after the yeast, and I added a little amount of glucose to feed them. It worked quite well, as the action of the yeast remained predominant, giving very nice yellow fruits and floral-honey flavours, underlined by a refreshing astringency and a nice acidity. To be honest, the latter could have been a bit more present to my taste—but this was a first trial.

"The grist was made of pale malt (55 percent), raw wheat (40 percent), and raw oat (5 percent). The mashing schedule was extremely simple compared to the ones used in the past: infusion method with four steps: 45° C for 20 minutes, 62° C for 45 minutes, 72° C for 30 minutes, and 78° C for 15 minutes (113/144/162/172° F). Knowing that the attenuation would be low, as well as the acidity level, I didn't want to get a beer too dextrinous, so it would remain refreshing. The gravity was 10.9 °P, the abv 3.4%. A long boil of three hours and 30 minutes added color, so at dark blond the beer makes one think to Peeterman rather than Blanche de Louvain. The hops were old Hallertau at the start of boiling and fresh Saaz at the end.

"We made this beer at Cantillon, and at Cantillon a beer has to be kept for a very long time in a wooden barrel—a local rule. So as I write these lines it is still there. It's not a lambic, which is a cool thing—it means we made something special. But for the real result, we'll have to wait for the bottling to happen. Next year (2010), I will repeat the experience in my own brewery, with a way shorter maturation time. We plan then to have a big Brussels White party."

took the idea to flash pasteurize its *wit* from German brewers. Hull said the Germans talked about denaturing the yeast cells, which helps stabilize flavor because it removes the danger of autolysis. In a broader sense flash pasteurizing also denatures the proteins, so they don't clump together and drop out of suspension because of gravity or because they are dragged down by yeast cells. (See page 29.) New Belgium, like other brewers selling cloudy beers, includes instructions on the bottle urging customers to swirl the final portion before pouring, thus tossing yeast and protein that have settled back into suspension.

"That's really important for these beers. It's all about the appearance," Hull said, "making it as close to white as you can get it."

Two Times White Is Still White

Phil Markowski, author of *Farmhouse Ales,* discovered *wit* beers while visiting Belgium in the 1980s. After he couldn't find them fresh back in the United States, he started making his own at home. His recipe won several awards, so he hauled it out after he became brewmaster at Southampton Publick House on Long Island. It bombed.

The following winter he brewed *Double White,* at 6.6 percent alcohol by volume strong but not "imperial," as a seasonal special, and customers lapped it up. It remained a seasonal until Southampton began to have its beers brewed under contract for distribution. *Double White* immediately outsold the other two brewed for wide distribution, *Southampton Secret,* brewed in the manner of a German-style *altbier,* and *Southampton IPA.* The brewery since has entered into a strategic alliance with Pabst Brewing that expanded distribution to fifteen states—and *Double White* remains the lead horse.

SOUTHAMPTON DOUBLE WHITE
Original Gravity: 1.065 (16 °P)
Alcohol by Volume: 6.6%
Apparent Degree of Attenuation: 78%
IBU: 18
Malts: Pilsener, unmalted wheat, acidulated malt, flaked oats
Adjuncts: Sucrose
Spices: Coriander, orange peel
Hops: Saaz, Magnum
Yeast: House yeast
Primary Fermentation: Yeast pitched at 68° F (20° C), rises to 71° F (22° C), 5 to 7 days
Secondary Fermentation: 32° F (0° C), 7 to 9 days
Also Noteworthy: Not bottle conditioned

Markowski oversees brewing *Double White* at the City Brewery in Latrobe, Pennsylvania, former home of Rolling Rock. There the brewing water has only moderate hardness, which seems to suit the beer. "I don't think of it as an edgy style. A soft water source is ideal," Markowski said, contrasting that to "Burtonizing" water to give an English ale the proper mineral firmness.

He uses a multistep infusion, including a protein rest, to make *Double White*, part of an effort to keep the beer as cloudy as possible. "That seems to me to be an essential character, and we've had some problems maintaining that." He adds oats to enhance permanent haze and uses a powdery yeast.

"We expect it has a four-month shelf life," he said. By then the beer will fall bright at room temperature, with the spice flavors fading. "It becomes more like a strong Belgian ale, like *Duvel*," Markowski said. "One gets more of a sense of the lean body and mouthfeel. Not necessarily for better or worse."

A Taste of Leuven?

Might Jolly Pumpkin *Calabaza Blanca* provide a hint of what a nineteenth century Belgian white beer in the region of Leuven tasted like? Those beers certainly had the lactic tartness of *Blanca,* but probably not the *Brettanomyces* character, because they were served young.

When the brewery first released *Calabaza Blanca,* only its third beer at the time, brewmaster Ron Jeffries was surprised by some of the complaints. "People would say white beers aren't supposed to be sour. They were supposed to be sweet, friendly, happy beers," he said. "For me this makes the beer infinitely more drinkable. Otherwise they can be a little flabby, a little sweet, a little cloying. The lactic adds tartness, the *Brett* dries it up, take away some of the sweetness."

JOLLY PUMPKIN CALABAZA BLANCA

Original Gravity: 1.045 (11.2 °P)
Alcohol by Volume: 4.8%
Apparent Degree of Attenuation: 82%
IBU: 15
Malts: Pilsener, wheat, unmalted wheat
Hops: Vanguard
Yeast: House yeast, variation of WL550
Primary Fermentation: Yeast pitched at 65° F (18° C), rises to 78 to 82° F (26 to 28° C), always fast fermentation
Secondary Fermentation: In oak tun, about 2 weeks
Also Noteworthy: Bottle conditioned

He uses both malted and unmalted wheat in *Calabaza Blanca*, mashing in about 147° to 149° F (64° to 65° C), pitching his yeast (a house version of WL550) at 65° F (18° C) and letting it free rise, usually to about 78 to 82° F (25° to 28° C). A relatively small beer (4.8 percent alcohol by volume), *Blanca* will near terminal gravity in less than two days. The identifying character comes from the two weeks or so the beer spends in Jolly Pumpkin's wood tuns, which are rich in wild yeasts.

Jeffries said *Blanca* tastes oaky and of wet wood when he and his staff bottle it, with prominent fresh orange and a bit of banana. As the wild strains go to work in the bottle, it develops more sour, dry notes, and the flavor turns from fresh, wet wood to sour wood. Unlike a *wit* that might be called delicate *Blanca* retains its lively character for at least two years in a bottle. However, the proteins drop out with time, and it will pour clear unless the yeast gets a good shake. "I'd get comments back from GABF judging that a white beer should not be filtered," Jeffries said. "I'd tell them to come to our brewery and find a filter."

Calabaza Blanca certainly broadens any definition of *wit* based on *Celis White*. "Five years ago, it didn't seem many people were making *wit*. Now I'm still seeing it growing," he said. "I'd say *wit* has come out of the shadows."

chapter five

A RECIPE FOR WIT

"I hated it. It was totally different from everything I had tasted before."
  -Brewer Jean-François Gravel, remembering his first taste of wit

Jean-François Gravel of Dieu du Ciel! in Montreal learned about contracting for hops following the shortages of 2007. Like other brewers he discovered that he sometimes ended up with more of a variety than he wanted. In the summer of 2009 he realized he had more Cascade—a hop he does not like all that much but ordered to back up his supply of Centennial and Amarillo—than he needed.

He created a beer he called *Cascade Blanche*, a *witbier* with about 25 bittering units, all from Cascade, including a large late dose for flavor and aroma and still more in the dry hop. He liked the way the citrusy notes of Cascade played off the coriander and orange peel.

It's not true this was the 417th *wit* Gravel had created. It only seems that way. Since he and his partners opened the Dieu du Ciel! brewpub in 1998 and followed with a separate microbrewery, Gravel has established a reputation for brewing extraordinary beers. Some, like *Péché Mortel Imperial Coffee Stout*, have earned a cult following far from Montreal. Still, the best way to appreciate the range is to settle beneath the chalkboard at the brewpub, which routinely includes about fifteen

Jean-François Gravel. (Photo courtesy of Dieu du Ciel!)

beers to choose from. At least one will likely be a Belgian-style *wit*.

As well as brewing what can be called a traditional *wit* Gravel has made, for starters, some that include apple juice, hibiscus flowers, ginger, mustard seeds, nutmeg, and star anise, and a strong version with cinnamon and nutmeg.

He hadn't yet discovered *wit* when, as a homebrewer, he made a *weizen* following instructions in Eric Warner's *German Wheat Beer*. He started with Unibroue's *Blanche de Chambly,* basically the reference beer for wheat in Quebec. "I hated it. It was totally different from everything I had tasted before," he said. In retrospect, he thinks that might have been because the bottle was old. Obviously he didn't give up on *wit*.

"To me, wheat has a very delicate, bready flavor with some acidity or refreshing tartness. I think the barley has more pronounced grain flavor and a sweeter perception," he said. "If you eat raw wheat and malted wheat, you will see the difference of texture right away, because the malted wheat is more crumbly and easy to crush. But the flavor difference between the unmalted and malted wheat is very subtle. The malted wheat will have a bit more . . . malty flavor."

He began using malted wheat in the grist at the brewpub, because what he can accomplish with step infusion there is limited. He said when he introduced wheat malt into his *wit* the fermentation character improved, and he attributes that to lower beta glucan levels and higher FAN (free amino nitrogen) levels. He believes that malted wheat may be even more important for a brewer limited to a single infusion.

When Gravel talks about "coriander punch" he is describing impact, not the "coriander soup" that Belgian purists complain about. Nonetheless, he doesn't hide his affection for the spice. "I have to say that I love coriander seeds, so I use a lot. I followed the guidelines from brewing books for my first versions and increased it slowly until I had the coriander punch I like," he said. "I use a lot less when I introduce other spices in other versions of *wit* beer."

He reminds novices that coriander provides citrusy aroma and flavor to *wit* beer, while orange peel lends a balancing herbal bitterness.

Original Gravity: 1.054 (13.5 °P)
Final Gravity: 1.013 (3.3 °P)
Alcohol by Volume: 5.5%
IBU: 14

Grain Bill:
Pale two-row 50%
Malted wheat 20%
Pregelatinized (torrified or flaked) wheat 30%
Rice hulls as needed

Mashing:
Mash at a ratio of 3.1 L/kg of grist (0.4 gallons per pound)
Mash in at 124° F (51° C) for 15 minutes
Saccharification at 145° F (63° C) for 30 minutes
Saccharification at 154° F (68° C) for 15 minutes
Mash out at 169 to 172° F (76 to 78° C)

For single step hold at 145° F (63° C) for 45 to 60 minutes. Sparge with very hot water, 176 to 180° F (80-82° C) to increase the temperature of the mash up to 158 to 169° F (70 to 76° C). Then run the sparge with 169 to 172° F (76 to 78° C) water until the end.

Hops: Mt. Hood, 60 minutes (15 IBU)
Spices: Fresh ground coriander 0.75g to 1.25 g/L
(0.1 to 1.25 ounces per gallon)
Orange peel 0.5 g/L (0.05 ounces per gallon)

Boil: 60 minutes

Yeast: Whitelabs WLP400 or WLP410 or Wyeast 3942 or 3944

Fermentation: 5 to 6 days at 73° F (23° C). Drop temperature to 50° F (10° C) for 24 hours, then to 32° F (0° C). Lager 10 to 15 days.

Bottling: Refermentation in the bottle

■■■ The Secret Spice: Fresh?

Pierre Celis was upholding a tradition among Belgian brewers of creating an air of mystery when he would at one moment deny using any spices other than coriander and Curaçao and in the next suggest a secret ingredient he would rather not reveal. Today in Portland, Maine, Allagash Brewing founder Rob Tod and head brewer Jason Perkins keep that spirit alive by smiling and laughing as they talk about the evening Tod's lips got a little loose and he revealed the secret spice in *Allagash White*.

Perhaps mystery is the secret ingredient. A better candidate could be "fresh." It depends on what a brewer expects from adjuncts. Gravel points out that he wants citrus from coriander and bitterness from orange peels. Others ask for citrus from orange and might blend a mixture of sweet and bitter.

Freshness, as in refreshing to drink, is one of the hallmarks of this style, and many commercial brewers appreciate that. "If your coriander isn't fresh, then it will have no aroma," said Derek Osborne, BJ's Restaurants director for research and development. He adds one ounce of freshly ground coriander per barrel to the award-winning *Nit Wit*. Likewise, Grady Hull at New Belgium Brewing orders his organic orange peel, lemon peel, and coriander only a week before he puts *Mothership Wit* on the brewing schedule. In Belgium, Bavik mills both orange peel and coriander just before using them.

Michael Jackson wrote that he tasted cumin in the Texas version of *Celis White*, but others have reporter chamomile. Still other brewers use ginger (including Jolly Pumpkin, although Ron Jeffries since has quit adding it to *Calabaza Blanca*), grains of paradise, and the dizzying number of additions Gravel has tried.

Randy Mosher provides a complete primer on spices in *Radical Brewing*. He points out a key difference in kinds of coriander, favoring the rugby-ball-shaped variety found in Indian markets.

PART III:
THE WEISS BEERS OF SOUTHERN GERMANY

chapter six

A FALLEN STYLE RETURNS TO GLORY

"In weissbier you have lots of different varieties of flavors. Different fruits, spices, phenolics. In lagers I find hops and malt."

– Hans-Peter Drexler

Brewmaster Hans-Peter Drexler stops talking about water treatment and takes a deep breath as he reaches the door to the fermentation room at Private Weissbierbrauerei G. Schneider & Sohn. He can smell what's on the other side and he's already smiling. "I love this," he says, throwing the door open to a floor with ten open fermentation tanks, each with a capacity of 32,869 liters (8,683 gallons). Billowing clouds of yeast fill six more open vats downstairs, the aroma totally intoxicating.

"This is the soul of the brewery," Drexler says. He walks between the big round fermenters as he talks about using slotted spoons to skim hop resins and trub off the top of the yeast. "The flavors are very hard and bitter," he says. "For me it is important to remove them." On his left, yeast climbs high in a tank filled with wort on its way to being the strong wheat *doppelbock* called *Aventinus*. On his right fermentation only recently started on what will be a batch of *Schneider Weisse Original*. A small hole opens in the middle of the yeast blanket, briefly revealing the wort below before closing again. It is alive.

Open fermentation tank at Weissbierbrauerei Schneider

Scores, even hundreds, of smaller breweries across Bavaria still employ open fermentation, but Schneider is the largest to make its wheat beers using traditional methods, including a decoction mash, open fermentation, and bottle conditioning with *speise* (see Chapter 7). Schneider produces 300,000 hectoliters a year (more than 250,000 barrels), while giants Erdinger, Paulaner, and Spaten all make more than a million.

SCHNEIDER WEISSE ORIGINAL
Original Gravity: 1.052 (12.8 °P)
Alcohol by Volume: 5.4%
Apparent Degree of Attenuation: 80%
IBU: 14
Malts: Pilsener, wheat, chocolate
Hops: Magnum, Hallertau Tradition
Yeast: House yeast
Primary Fermentation: Yeast pitched at 61° F (16° C), rises to 71 to 73° F (22 to 23° C), 5 days
Also Noteworthy: Bottle conditioned with *speise*

Earlier Drexler considered a question put to him as a brewing scientist. Were he told Schneider was about to expand its production to a million hectoliters and he had no choice but to ferment his beer in cylindrical-conical tanks, could he brew beers with the exact same flavors as those Schneider currently makes? He shrugged. "I didn't try it," he said, giving himself more time for thought. "I think if you had a beer from an open tank I can taste the difference."

Years ago Schneider did tests on the mechanism of aeration and open fermentation. "We found the flavors of 4-vinyl guaiacol (clove) are much stronger if you have a little more aeration," he said "This is a typical flavor for our brewery."

Schneider is no newcomer to brewing wheat beers. In the up and down and up again history of German *weissbier,* the brewery has been around for the last two eras, playing an important historic role at a time when *weissbier* seemed on the verge of becoming extinct. Although we know that something akin to wheat beer was made in what is now Germany at least 2,800 years ago, the partly cloudy beer tasting of banana and cloves we call *weissbier* goes back more like 500 years and probably originated in Bohemia. In a curious turn of history the first wheat beers in Bavaria were known as "Bohemian" and the first lagers in what was previously ale-brewing Bohemia were called "Bavarian." Duke Hans VI von Degenberg and his family established the first recorded *weissbier* brewery in about 1500 in the town of Schwarzach, not far from what is now the German-Czech border. Early on the brewery made "Behemisch Wiss Pir" (Bohemian white beer).

What followed has been well documented elsewhere. Basically, wheat beer from the Degenbergs sold so well that after a bit of royal tussling the Wittelsbachs, Bavaria's ruling family since 1180, turned brewing wheat beer into a lucrative ducal monopoly. After claiming full rights to brew or license *weissbier* in 1602, Maximilian I (and later his successors) built breweries across Bavaria. *Weissbier* flourished during the seventeenth century and much of the eighteenth, with sales peaking in 1730, before *braunbier* reasserted itself and wheat beer sales tumbled. The monopoly ended in 1798 when noblemen and monasteries were granted the right to brew, and by 1812 only two *weissbier*-specific breweries still operated. To the north Berliner *weisse* enjoyed substantial success, but in the south *weissbier* could barely be found.

In 1872 the first Georg Schneider laid the groundwork for a *weissbier* revival—though it was still almost a century away and Georg Schneider V would be in charge of the family brewery by then—when he acquired the rights to brew from King Ludwig II. The transaction extended *weissbier* brewing rights to all commoners, not just Schneider. He first brewed in Munich, in the location that's now the Weisses Brauhaus, a delightful restaurant/bier hall. Schneider & Sohn acquired the Weisses Brauhaus in Kelheim, north of Munich and southwest of Nürnberg, in 1927. After a fire destroyed the Munich facility in 1946, the company moved all brewing operations to Kelheim, later rebuilding the Munich Brauhaus as a restaurant.

Even in its home state of Bavaria *weissbier* claimed only 3 percent of the beer market as recently as 1960, when overall wheat beer production in Germany was less than 500,000 hectoliters.

	Original Gravity SG (Plato)	Alcohol by Volume	Apparent Extract	Bitterness (IBU)	Volumes CO_2 (grams/ liter)
Paulaner Hefe-Weissbier	1.050 (12.5 °P)	5.5%	84%	13	3 (6)
Paulaner Hefe-Weissbier Dunkel	1.050 (12.4 °P)	5.4%	82%	13	3 (6)
Paulaner Hefe-Weissbier Kristallklar	1.048 (11.8 °P)	5.2%	83%	10	3.15 (6.3)
Paulaner Hefe-Weissbier Leicht	1.031 (7.8 °P)	3.2%	80%	10	3.35 (6.7)
Franziskaner Hefeweissbier	1.047 (11.7 °P)	5%	84%	12	3.5 (7)
Franziskaner Hefeweissbier Dunkel	1.047 (11.65 °P)	4.9%	81%	12	3.5 (7)
Franziskaner Kristalweissbier	1.047 (11.75 °P)	5.1%	85%	15.5	3.7 (7.4)
Franziskaner Hefeweissbier Leicht	1.030 (7.5 °P)	2.9%	75%	12	Not given

By 1970 sales had doubled, then they tripled between 1970 and 1980, and doubled again during the 1980s to more than 6.5 million hectoliters in 1990. The pace of growth has since slowed, but production reached almost 12 million hectoliters (more than 10 million barrels) in 2008, with nearly 90 percent of that sold in Germany. The success of wheat beers stands in stark contrast to overall German beer production, which began declining annually in 1996. Large breweries, expanding several times over, and smaller ones benefited equally. Not surprisingly, many more breweries began making wheat beers, and wheat beer specialists expanded their lineups. When Drexler went to work at Schneider in 1982 he oversaw the production of two beers, *Schneider Original* and *Aventinus*. Today Schneider sells eight year-round wheat beers, including *Schneider Weisse Alkoholfrei*, and occasional special beers.

Wheat beer accounted for about 9 percent of German beer production in 2008 but 36 percent in Bavaria, more than any other style. Broken down further, 43 percent of beer brewed in the south of Bavaria was *weissbier*. In northern Bavaria, including the Bamberg area, Pilsener remains most popular (35 percent share versus 20 percent for *weissbier*).

Little wonder that Walter König of the Bavarian Brewers Association talks about Bavarian "wheat beer competence," somehow managing not to sound arrogant when he says, "People know if they want a wheat beer there should be blue and white (the ubiquitous colors representing Bavaria) on it."

German beer writer Werner Oblaski, who refers to his hometown of Munich as "The World's Capital of Beer," agrees. "*Hefeweizen* is brewed very rarely in Northern Germany. You have Flensburger and Veltins, for example and—from Frankfurt—the famous Schöfferhofer; this is well known all over Germany and perhaps other parts of Europe because of the very clever advertising, not because of the quality," he wrote in an email. "Germans consider very well the differences between a *hefeweizen* from the south, that means Bavaria, and the other countries. It is an invention of the south and it will be connected mainly with the south of Germany."

Sylvia Kopp, a beer writer and certified beer sommelier, points to specific differences in flavor. "You might distinguish more phenolic flavors in Bavarian *weissbier*, while *weizens* from breweries in the northern half of the country tend to be more bitter and straight (as a lager)," she wrote in an email. "On the whole, beer enthusiasts are rather aware of this, but most of the beer consumers don't really care. They buy what is available and follow brands."

She sees regional difference extending to awareness of certain breweries. "Northern Germans do for sure know Erdinger and Paulaner, some might know Schneider and Maisel but haven't ever heard of Gutmann, Unertl, or Karg. Southerners know the small breweries and could be more likely to prefer them," she wrote. "On the whole, I think, there is a tendency to perceive the smaller ones as more authentic because they are more tied to their region."

Hyper-growth beginning in the 1960s generated change, although many of the larger breweries won't discuss much of that in detail. They hold recipes, as well as the processes they use, which reportedly have changed, proprietary. A variety of industry members will say, off the record, that some breweries that once used a decoction mash no longer do, that closed fermenters (often cylindrical-conical tanks) have replaced open ones, that flash pasteurization (which denatures the proteins so they stay in suspension) is a shortcut to haze stability, and that yeast in the bottle doesn't guarantee a beer is traditionally bottle conditioned.

Different breweries reveal different aspects of how they brew. Not talking about others doesn't necessarily mean that these brewers are trying to hide anything; just that one will classify some details privileged that others don't. For instance, Munich's Paulaner Brewery considers some of its packaging procedures proprietary, but acknowledges that although yeast makes it appear cloudy, *Paulaner Hefe-Weissbier* is not bottle conditioned.

Paulaner still employs a decoction mash, but Spaten, which brews *Fransizkaner Hefeweissbier*, abandoned decoction in 2000. Spaten uses a single-infusion mash at 62° C (144° F), saving on labor, time, and energy costs. Not long after he took charge of brewing operations at Spaten in 2005, Dr. Jörg Lehmann said the decision came after a series of blind taste tests in which participants couldn't tell the difference. "The malt quality has improved very much," he explained.

Josef Ernst, Lehmann's predecessor at Spaten, added the brewery might make changes for other reasons. "You can't use the same processes as you did twenty years ago," he said. "Consumers want a different beer."

In a one-room museum deep within the Weissbierbrauerei Schneider, a book containing the original Schneider recipe sits under glass. While the formula for *Schneider Weisse Original* from 1864 might be basically the same, the way in which it is executed certainly isn't. "Fifty years ago, the beer was sold around the chimney," Drexler says. Now it is sold around the world, but each of the modifications made so the beer could travel farther and remain fresh longer reflects a certain determination to keep the process traditional.

For instance, Schneider installed a new system to generate and control *speise* for bottle conditioning. Rather than using wort from a newly brewed batch, as Schneider did in the past and many other breweries still do, Schneider has what's essentially a separate *speise* recipe, hopped a little bit differently than its beer and made to a slightly different strength. It's added inline during bottling. "The amount of *speise* is critical," Drexler said. "You cannot use too much."

Additionally, in 1993 Schneider installed a yeast propagation system that produces fresh yeast for almost every batch of Schneider beers. You may have seen pictures of workers skimming yeast from Schneider fermenters and thought it was destined for future batches. Almost never— only the stronger *Aventinus* is fermented with a second generation, because it takes a little more oomph to take on the 1.076 (18.5 °P) beast.

"The idea was to reduce the risk for contamination. Sometimes we had problems with the microbiology when we used more generations," he says. "If you have every time a new generation, the yeast is going through the brewery and out."

Drexler scrunches his eyebrows, perhaps thinking about what a bottle of *Weisse Original* that left Bavaria eight months ago and traveled 6,000 often hot miles to a beer store somewhere in the American Southwest must face. He opens his hands and gestures as he speaks. "One of the big things about this brewery, all the time we work at 20 Centigrade (68° F)," he says. "The microbiology is very difficult to keep at a low level."

Visitors bottle their own beer at the end of a tour. (Photo courtesy of Schneider & Sohn.)

SCHNEIDER AVENTINUS

Original Gravity: 1.076 (18.5 °P)
Alcohol by Volume: 8.2%
Apparent Degree of Attenuation: 82%
IBU: 16
Malts: Pilsener, wheat, chocolate
Hops: Magnum, Hallertau Tradition
Yeast: House yeast
Primary Fermentation: Yeast pitched at 61° F (16° C), rises to 71 to 73° F (22 to 23° C), 7 days
Also Noteworthy: Bottle conditioned with *speise*

Both *Original* and *Aventinus* contain 60 percent wheat, with Pilsener making up most of the barley malt. *Original* has 1 percent chocolate malt and *Aventinus* somewhat more. Local farmers provide an increasing percentage of the grain, both barley and wheat, while the hops come from the nearby Hallertau region. About half are contracted with individual farmers and half with brokers.

"To me the raw ingredients are very important. I like to go talk to the farmers. To me they are doing the hard work ... giving us good materials," Drexler said.

A step-and-decoction mash lasts about 3 hours, and it takes more than 3½ hours more to lauter into a special wide tank. Schneider mashes-in for 10 minutes at 35° C (95° F), then conducts a 10-minute rest at 45° C (113° F). Research has found this is a key temperature for creation of ferulic acid, which, when it interacts with Schneider's yeast, creates 4-vinyl guaiacol, giving Schneider's beers a clovelike phenolic note that's part of the brewery's signature flavor.

Ferulic Acid Rest and Flavor Perception

Time of ferulic acid rest (113° F/45° C)	0 minutes	10 minutes	>25 minutes
Phenolic	1.2	2.1	3.3
Estric	4.1	3.4	2.6
Yeasty	1.8	2.6	2.8

Source: Ausgewählte Kapitel der Brauereitechnologie

Schneider shortens the protein rest at 50° C (122° F) to 10 minutes to avoid degrading the proteins and damaging head retention. (Were you to follow this schedule but adjust the ferulic acid rest, you would also want to change the protein rest appropriately.) After a 5-minute rest at 64° C (147° F) the brewers pull a one-third decoction. That is heated to 67° C (152° F) for 10 minutes, to 70° C (158° F) for 20 minutes, and then to 95° C (203° F) for 5 minutes. When the decoction is transferred back, the mash sets at 75° C (167° F).

Schneider acidifies its wort during the boil, because "if wort is too clean we get a neutral *weissbier*." The brewers take a special strain of *Lactobacillus* and add it to wort drawn from the lauter tank. This mixture with a pH of 3.0 goes into the boiling kettle, improving the quality of the fermentation. Drexler finds his beer also tastes crisper. Magnum hops are added at the beginning of the one-hour boil and Hallertau Tradition with 10 minutes left.

Drexler calls the yeast "a very old strain," and says, "I don't know what time it is from." Schneider's brewers pitch 6 million to 7 million cells per milliliter, but a) that's particularly vital yeast straight from the

■■■ The Lemon Garnish: For Tourists Only

To celebrate 400 years of wheat brewing on the site in Kelheim that's now home to Private Weissbierbrauerei G. Schneider & Sohn, the brewery created a special beer called *1608*, a little stronger than *Schneider Weisse Original*. Brewmaster Hans-Peter Drexler hopped it at a slightly higher rate than a typical *weissbier* and with a newish German hop called Saphir, which added a bit of a citrus flavor.

"They say it was a Bavarian tradition to serve *weiss* with lemon," Drexler explained, referring to the practice as if it were a bit of ancient history not everybody believes existed.

Ask an American beer drinker why the bartender just hung a lemon on a glass of *hefeweizen* and the answer likely would be, "Because that's the way the Germans do it." Wrong. Maybe once upon a time, but certainly not now. "Oh no, no, that is something that was done in the 1980s, I remember, with *kristall weizen*," beer sommelier and writer Sylvia Kopp wrote in an email. "Now it is not accepted behavior."

Not in Bavaria, that is. The practice remains common in the United States and brings little joy to Greg Zaccardi, founder of High Point Brewing in New Jersey. "I don't think we need it. But otherwise I tell people it is up to them," he said. "After a few beers I tend to get more surly and tell them it's beer, it's not tea.

"We design the beer to have the right kind of balance. We want it to have the middle notes, the high notes, the lower ones. The right symphonic volume. I think our beer has the right flavors without it. That said . . . people can do what they want."

In his autobiography Bert Grant, who started the first post-Prohibition brewpub in the United States, was more emphatic about lemon. "That's fine for improving the flavor of some of the very mild American-style versions, but you don't need a lemon or lime when you drink *Grant's HefeWeizen*. My beer's got enough flavor from the wheat malt and above-average hopping. Besides, I'm seeing a lot of *hefeweizen* drinkers these days who have joined the 'NFL' team—the first word is "No," the last is "Lemon," and you can figure out the one in the middle!"

Michael Jackson once suggested the lemon garnish might be linked to the practice of serving juice or syrup with Berliner *weisse*, that it was visually appealing and highlighted the refreshing character of wheat beer. In a 1991 column in "What's Brewing" he wrote: "When I first encountered South German wheat beers, in the early to mid-1960s, they were regarded as an old-fashioned, rustic style, favored by old ladies with large hats. The beer was at that time customarily garnished with a slice of lemon.

"People have told me the lemon was to mask the taste of the uneven products made at that time by unscientific country brewers; I do not believe that. Some of the wilder wheat beers might taste odd to the uninitiated, but not to people who grew up with them.

"I have also heard it said that the lemon reduced the foam to manageable proportions, but why would anyone want to flatten a naturally sparkling drink?

"I believe the lemon accentuated the tart, refreshing character of the beer, and I am sorry that it is so rarely seen in Germany today."

Before you decide to quote Jackson and ask for a lemon in a Bavarian beer, consider this thought from Munich-based beer journalist Werner Oblaski: "Lemon with *hefeweizen* you only will see when Aussies and Kiwis drink it."

propagator, and b) they are considering increasing the count for a faster start and greater microbiological safety. Fermentation begins at 61 to 63° F (16 or 17° C) and will reach 72° F (22° C) in the open vessels, lasting five days for *Original* and seven for *Aventinus.*

The finished beer will be blended in a buffer tank with other beer ready to package, resting overnight. "If we wait too long, the fermentation starts in the tank," Drexler explained. It must begin in the bottle or it will lose carbon dioxide. *Speise* is added inline along with yeast. Schneider targets 1 million to 2 million cells per milliliter in the bottle, which will create 3.5 volumes of CO_2 (7 grams per liter). Conditioning takes three weeks, the first at 70° F (21° C) and the next two at 50° F (10° C), all of that needed to get rid of diacetyl created by the process.

A collection of old equipment dominates the balcony overlooking the brewery's high-tech bottling line. Some of these contraptions hold one bottle, others dozens. Most are for decoration, but an important one remains in working order. At the conclusion of a brewery tour each visitor fills a single bottle with flat beer and flips the top closed. They take it home with instructions about how to complete bottle conditioning so that in three weeks they've got a fully carbonated *Schneider Weisse Original.*

They might choose to wait longer were they allowed to bottle *Aventinus,* the oldest wheat *doppelbock* (or *weizenbock*) in Bavaria, first brewed in 1907. Although most *Aventinus,* like the *Original,* is ready to drink in three weeks, about 250 cases of the beer are set aside to age in an old ice cellar for three years, destined to be exported to the

United States and sold as vintage *Aventinus*. The clever bit of marketing has earned a certain amount of attention, which must amuse those near Kelheim.

"The people here in this region always said you have to keep *Aventinus* in a cold cellar for two years," Drexler said. "That's the real *Aventinus*."

Drexler might be late for lunch with his boss, Georg Schneider VI (father of Georg VII, who was born in 1995), but the *Weisse Original* has poured a little cold and we must wait until it's properly warm. As it warms, the phenolics come up rather quickly, the experience more than a little like approaching the door to the fermentation room.

The first time I visited the Schneider brewery, Drexler talked about why breweries would abandon open fermentation, particularly as production increases. "It is not easy to keep consistency. Each bottle is its own system," he said. Watching him lift his glass to his nose, it's obvious why Schneider hasn't.

"It is a very traditional system, and we are a little bit proud of it."

chapter seven

BAVARIAN TRADITION WITH A WYOMING ACCENT

"There's nothing about the quality of the ingredients in the Reinheits-gebot . . . nothing about temperature or times."

– Eric Toft, Private Landbrauerei Schönram

Half a rainbow hangs over chestnut red-and-white Pinzgauer cattle, once bred for work at Bavarian breweries, grazing beside the road leading to the village of Petting/Schönram and Private Landbrauerei Schönram. Inside the brewery laboratory Eric Toft hoists test tubes and scribbles notes about beer that will be filtered today.

In his adjoining office a large map of Wyoming, where Toft grew up, hangs over a conference table. Another nearby shows the hop yards in the nearby Hallertau region, where farmers he knows personally grow his hops. He gestures out the window to the Alps and toward where he and his family went hiking yesterday, explaining the fresh sunburn on his nose.

A little later he introduces Michael Schoenauer, his predecessor as brewmaster, when Schoenauer stops by unannounced, apologizing because he has brewed a batch of beer at home and miscalculated how much *speise* he needs for bottle conditioning. He wants only a half liter, but since he can wait a day Toft suggests he come back and get fresh first runnings tomorrow. Schoenauer smiles and nods, acknowledging a particular attention to detail they share.

Toft is a man in full, discontent this October morning only when the conversation turns to bureaucratic obstacles German brewers face. He's irritated about the recently rejected application that would have granted Hallertau hops status as an appellation (like Dijon mustard, or, more importantly, Czech Saaz hops). He often says "we" when comparing his own German government to the Czech leadership, which has actively opposed higher beer taxes, unlike the Germans.

"I consider myself German," he says when asked about this choice of words. He grew up in Wyoming and went to college at the Colorado School of Mines but moved to Germany to study beer in 1987, and after graduating from the Weihenstephan school of brewing has lived either in Belgium or Germany. He met his wife, Evi, when they were both students at Weihenstephan. She did her apprenticeship at the teaching and trial brewery, which made side brands for the Bavarian state brewery of Weihenstephan, including *Dunkles Weissbier* and occasionally *Helles Weissbier.*

With the exception of Toft himself, the farthest from the brewery anybody who works there grew up is about five kilometers (three miles). He was one of sixty applicants for the job in 1997, after Schoenauer announced he would retire because of health reasons. Toft had been working for nearly six years as second brewmaster at a larger brewery nearby. "I'd always revered (Schönram)," Toft says. "I was one of the few younger brewers who thought open fermentation was cool."

Bernard Kuhn, who owns the nearby Weissbräu Hotel, recalls that Schönram owner Alfred Oberlindober had said he would only hire a Bavarian brewer.

Turns out he did.

Schönram was strictly a lager brewery before first making its *Schönramer Festweisse* in 2005. It produced about 46,000 hectoliters (39,000 barrels) in 2008 but feels larger than comparable-sized ale breweries because of the extra space needed for fermentation and lagering rooms. (Recall that *Schneider Weisse Original* gets bottled right after primary fermentation, eliminating the need for an entire layer of tanks.)

Toft faces an ongoing dilemma. Production has nearly doubled over the past ten years at Schönram (whose beers bear the motto: "Das grosse Bier aus der kleinen Brauerei," or, "the big beer from the small brewery"), at the same time German beer sales tumbled annually. Which trend should he bet on in planning for future growth? "I could just raise my temperatures a bit," he said, because that would speed up how fast a batch moves through the system. "The Reinheitsgebot (Germany's 'beer purity' law) says nothing about temperatures and times. But I won't do that." In fact, his fermentations start cooler than most and remain cooler. Then he lagers his beers longer. For the sake of comparison, consider Berliner-Kindl-Schultheiss Brauerei in Berlin. The multimedia presentation shown during a tour proudly explains that despite additional energy costs the brewery chills *Berliner Pilsner* for two weeks before bottling. *Schönramer Pils* lagers six weeks after primary.

Schönram also uses more hops than most Bavarian breweries, selling beers as rich in hop character as bitterness because they include only aroma hops from the Hallertau region. Brewers skim the open fermenters—for lagers as well as the wheat beer—daily, further enhancing the beers' smooth impression. Schoenauer designed the new fermenters in 1995. They look like something you would have seen on the once futuristic cartoon show "The Jetsons" (see color page V). They are shallow, with a height-to-diameter ratio of less than one-to-one. Each has a door that locks in place so they can be cleaned as easily as cylindro-conical tanks.

Not until 2003 could Toft segregate top and bottom fermentation and begin thinking about brewing a *weiss*. A local historian says he has found proof that wheat beer was brewed locally in the 1640s, but Schönram didn't begin brewing until 1780. Toft created *Festweisse* to celebrate the brewery's 225th anniversary with the idea it could be strictly a one-time offering or turn into a regular.

German law requires a "fest" beer be comparable to 12.5 °P (1.050) or stronger, and while the wort originally knocks out at 12.3 or 12.4 °P, *Festweisse* qualifies because Toft uses higher-gravity first runnings in his *speise*. A measure of Vienna malt makes it dark enough to be classified as a *Bernsteinfarbenes hefeweizen*. *Bernsteinfarbe* means amber color, and the category was created to accommodate the range of color between *helles* and *dunkels*, as many wheat beers fall in that range, most notably *Schneider Weisse Original*. *Schönram Festweisse* medaled in the category in the 2008 European Beer Star competition, judged in Germany.

Because the first runnings aren't hopped, they also dilute the final IBU, allowing Toft a little more microbiological protection during primary fermentation. He calculated the final IBU in his first batches at 16, but brought that down to 12 or 13 as he became comfortable using less hops. Many brewers in Bavaria have lowered bitterness levels in *hefeweizens* to 10 or 11. He adds Hersbrucker hops twice, 75 percent of the load 10 minutes into a one-hour boil and the rest with 10 minutes remaining.

The grist contains 65 percent wheat (originally equal parts dark wheat and light), Vienna, and a bit of Caradunkel. Now he uses only light wheat, because he's more likely to get the lower protein levels he wants. He adds the Caradunkel to compensate for the drop in color.

Many American brewers know Toft because he represents the Hallertau Hop Growers Association each year at the Craft Brewers Conference. He's a hop judge for a major German competition every fall and was elected to the board of scientific advisers for the Society of Hop Research in 2009.

He buys his hops directly from farmers, although purchasing some through co-ops offers security in case a single yard is wiped out by bad weather. "I give them what I would pay the trade. It takes time to get to know the farmers personally and build up a sound relationship," he said.

He considers knowing the varieties of barley and wheat that go into his malt just as important, favoring barley varieties like Barke and Stepha that are becoming harder to find because they are less efficient to grow. "What it comes down to for the farmer is yield, so I pay more," he said.

He would like to be able to do the same for wheat but doesn't brew enough beer to assure he'll get the same variety all the time. "I prefer Atlantis, but I have analysis of different batches sent to me before I order and base my decision on that," he said. "The main thing for me is low protein modification. I don't care too much about the total protein, which is usually around 11 to 12 percent. I will go to 12.5 percent but don't like to go above that."

To brew *Festweisse*, Toft mashes in at 104° F (40° C), then heats it to 109° F (43° C) and lets it rest for 8 minutes to release ferulic acid. He then heats the mash to 149° F (65° C), resting it for 25 minutes before separating the mash into two parts. The size of each is calculated so that when they are reunited the mash temperature will be 171° F (77° C).

SCHONRÄMER FESTWEISSE
Original Gravity: 1.052 (12.8 °P)
Alcohol by Volume: 5.8%
Apparent Degree of Attenuation: 84%
IBU: 12-13
Malts: Pilsener, wheat, Vienna, Caradunkel
Hops: Hersbrucker
Yeast: From another brewery
Primary Fermentation: Yeast pitched at 64° F (18° C), rises to 73° F (23° C), 5 days
Secondary Fermentation: 35° F (2° C), 2 weeks
Also Noteworthy: Bottle conditioned with *speise*

Because Schönram has a two-vessel brew house, the brewers pump the portion not to be decocted (the larger part) into the lauter tun. The smaller portion that remains behind is heated to 162° F (72° C) and rests for 10 minutes. It's heated to a boil for 5 minutes. This portion gets pumped into the lauter tun until the temperature is 162° F (72° C), resting again for 8 minutes, while a portion of the decocted mash remains behind in the mash tun/kettle.

After the 8-minute rest he pumps everything into the lauter tun to reach a final temperature of 171° F (77° C).

He follows a similar mash regime, including a single decoction, for all his beers, but will mash-in anywhere between 113 and 140° F (45 and 60° C) and vary the rests depending on the malt. He always mashes-in the wheat beer at 104° F (40° C) for the ferulic acid rest and always heats through the proteolytic temperatures to get as little protein degradation as possible, but will vary the rests between 144 and 154° F (62 and 68° C) depending on the makeup of the malt.

Fermentation begins at 64° F (18° C), and within 6 or 7 hours the fermenter looks as if it is boiling. Brewers skim off yeast two to four times in the next 36 hours, and fermentation peaks at 73° F (23° C).

After 5 days, the last 36 to 48 hours of that cooling to conditioning temperature, they transfer the beer into an unbunged lagering tank, where it sits for 2 weeks at 36° F (2° C). By then no yeast should remain in suspension. The beer is bottled with *speise* (see pages 103-104), and bottle conditioning takes 2 weeks.

"I wanted the cloviness, esteriness to start," Toft said, tasting his beer. "The velvety full body you get with the grist combination and through bottle conditioning. I would like to have more on the estery side. That's hard with the Vienna; the higher solubles cut down the esters. But I want honest color."

Toft and his family live in an apartment—it comes with the job, as well as 120 liters of beer a month—on the second floor of the brewery's restaurant. The building dates to the 1700s, was the first postal stop between Salzburg and Munich, and the story goes that Napoleon once spent the night (sounds much like our "Washington slept here" stories).

His commute takes thirty seconds, a minute if he lingers to look at the mountains. "This is my mentality down here," he says, talking about hiking, hunting, and fishing, describing Bavaria as the Wyoming of Germany. "They speak a different language. The local dialect is easier for me than high German. . . . Nobody thinks it's weird I'm from Wyoming."

Tomorrow he will be off to the Hallertau region to judge hops in an annual competition. He knows the roads, and the farmers along the way, well.

"I can say my hops are from him, my barley is from there," he says. "I can show up at the door with a crate of beer and have dinner."

Meet the Other Schneider

Listening to Josef Schneider talk about brewing wheat beers could make you start to think it is simple.

Does he worry about haze stability?

"You brew the beer right, you serve it fresh, it is not a problem."

Would he consider making a beer without using a decoction mash? (The look on his face indicated just how crazy he thought this question was, but he answered anyway.)

"Bavarian beer must have more malt flavor. You must cook it long to make it that way. Otherwise you have Warsteiner . . . or American beer."

Why is open fermentation important for his beer?

Looking like a man who had just stepped on a carton of rotten eggs he pinched his nose. "This must come out."

Why does he bottle condition all his weissbier, rather than offer some of it on draft as well?

"It's like sex and Champagne, worth the bother."

Schneider owns Brauereigasthof Schneider, as his son Matthias will some day. A brewery has operated on the same site in Essing since 1640 and been owned by the Schneiders since 1887. This can cause some confusion because the internationally famous Schneider & Sohn brewery is located about five miles up the road in Kelheim.

For good reason, Josef Schneider stamps "Kleines Brauhaus im Altmühl" on his crates. Essing is a sliver of a town, squeezed between the Altmühl River and rocky cliffs. Castle ruins overlook the town, which is popular with hikers, cyclists, and those who ride the river on tour boats. Schneider brews about fifty times during a year, some batches yielding 30 hectoliters and others less, with wheat beers accounting for 60 percent of production.

He follows a step-and-decoction regimen that is common in the region (45/52/63/72° C, with the decoction at 63° C, which translates to 113/126/145/162° F), and still uses a grant during lautering. His *Weizenbier* includes 60 percent wheat malt ("I tried others. This is best."), 12 percent dark Munich, 3 percent acidulated malt, 10 percent Carahell, 10 percent dark malt (600 EBC) and 5 percent Pilsener malt. He adds Hallertau pellets at the beginning of a 90-minute boil, targeting 12 IBU.

Fermentation begins at 59° F (15° C) and rises to 68 to 69° F (20 or 21° C) in 4 to 5 days in square open fermenters. The wheat rests then conditions for just 2 or 3 days at close to freezing and is ready for bottling with *speise* taken from the most recent brew, regardless of style. Describing the process Schneider walks under an arch (the only part of the brewery to survive a fire in 1870), out the door, and points to a truck parked beside the brewery. He brews *Weizenbier* when the weather is moderate, so the enclosed back of the truck makes a perfect spot for bottle conditioning.

Schneider's son, Matthias, attended brewing school and then worked for Paulaner in China before returning home in 2008. He's anxious to talk about marketing and his plans to expand production. This stands in contrast to his father. "Our job is the restaurant and guest houses," he said, gesturing toward them with his right hand. "This is our hobby," he said, opening his left so that had I taken a photo at the moment, the brewery would have appeared to be sitting in his palm. He laughed loudly.

The Beers Are Smoked, The Wheat Isn't

Schneider also brews a smoked wheat beer eight or nine times a year for Brauerei Spezial. Schneider simply uses smoked malt that Spezial, one of two breweries in Bamberg to still smoke its own malt, provides. Schneider replaces the 12 percent portion of Munich malt in his *Weizenbier* with 12 percent smoked barley malt, otherwise brewing the beer exactly the same way.

Neither *Spezial Weissbier* nor *Schlenkerla Rauchweizen*, a smokier beer also made in Bamberg, seeks to approximate the ancient Grätzer style (pages 168-169). Heller Bräu, which brews Schlenkerla beers just up the hill from the famous tavern, began selling its *weizen* in 1998. "It was my father's decision," said Matthias Trum, who, like five generations of Trums before him who ran the brewery, lives above the tavern. "We didn't want to do it because it was fashionable but because it was historically correct."

The Trums decided to brew the beer because tavern regulars asked for it. "A lot of younger people. Bamberg is a student town," Trum said. "Well, we thought wheat beers have been around a long time, and so has open kilning (over smoky fires), so if you did a wheat beer it would have been smoked." If Trum is correct then it would seem all *weissbiers* might once have tasted of smoke.

Heller Bräu uses 50 percent barley malt it smokes itself and 50 percent unsmoked wheat malt in *Rauchweizen*. The beer gets all its color from the smoked malt. "When we did the first batch we were surprised to be that close to the *Schneider (Weisse Original)* color," Trum said. Otherwise, it is produced much as other wheat beers in the region, fermentation starting at 64° F (18° C) and rising to 72° F (22° C) in open vessels over the course of three days. It spends a couple of days settling and is bottled with *speise*.

Compared to the flagship *Aecht Schlenkerla Rauchbier,* which is brewed with all smoked malt, the *Rauchweizen* seems tame. Geoff Larson and Ray Daniels wrote in *Smoked Beers* that "the smoke tends to quickly submerge in the banana and clove *weizen* flavors that appropriately dominate a beer in this style." Trum agrees that the smoke character tends to fade. "After two or three pints," he said, beginning to smile. "That's what Franconians call a couple of sips."

An Open Fermentation Policy

When the press release went out in March 2009 that said Sierra Nevada Brewing would stop selling its *Unfiltered Wheat Beer,* fermented with its prototypical and neutral American ale yeast, and begin brewing a German-inspired *hefeweizen,* fermented with a Bavarian yeast, Bill Manley's email box filled quickly. Half those writing loved the idea, the brewery's communications director said, but the rest were downright mad because they loved that old wheat. They should have told more friends, because the Americanized wheat was a laggard for the seventeen years it was on the market.

Not so with *Kellerweis.* "We struggled to keep up with demand right out of the gate," Manley said, three months after Sierra Nevada began selling it in June.

It might be years before we see if *Kellerweis* does for *weizen* beers what *Blue Moon White* did for *wit.* Scott Jennings, for whom the beer is a labor of love, understands that. "It's a beer that's not for everyone. It's not beer in a way a lot of Americans think of beer," said Jennings, who runs Sierra Nevada's research and development brewery.

"I have a personal interest in *weizen.* The beers are beautifully simplistic on one level. I've learned from our work they are really hard to get right," he said. "The beer is so dependent on everything coming out right, the yeast character, the brew house character."

The brewers at Sierra Nevada don't do things half way. Jennings began working on a traditional *hefeweizen* in 2006, one 10-barrel pilot batch at a time. "We started to dissect it, change small things. Material and brew house changes, trying various mashing regimens, testing different wheat varieties, different yeast strains."

SIERRA NEVADA KELLERWEIS
Original Gravity: 1.052 (12.8 °P)
Alcohol by Volume: 4.8%
Apparent Degree of Attenuation: 71%
IBU: 15
Malts: Two-row pale, wheat, Munich
Hops: Perle, Sterling
Yeast: Bavarian
Primary Fermentation: Yeast pitched at 62° F (17° C), rises to 70° F (21° C), 5 days
Secondary Fermentation: Tanks chilled to 30° F (-1° C), 7 days

They found the yeast they wanted by chance. "One of our techs brought back some bottles from Gutmann, a beer hard to find even in Germany, and we cultured the yeast out of that," Manley said. Brauerei Gutmann is located in Tittung, about forty miles east of Kelheim (Schneider & Sohn), in a swath of Bavaria where *weizens* taste spicier than those to the south.

They kept working on the beer at the same time the brewery considered other possible replacements for the red-label American wheat. "We came to a crossroads," Jennings said. "We'd developed a couple of methods. We're not set up as a wheat beer brewery so we improvised and came up with a complex solution to a complex problem." When the decision was made to make *Kellerweis* the new full-time beer, Jennings, Sierra Nevada founder Ken Grossman, brewmaster Steve Dresler, and assistant brewmaster Bart Whipple headed to Germany.

"We wanted to see what else maybe we could do. Mostly yeast handling, fermentation schedule," Jennings said. They visited Brauerei Gutmann, Schneider & Sohn, Brauerei Aying, and the Andechs Monastery brewery on the Holy Mountain southwest of Munich. At Andechs brewing happens in a modern facility at the base of the hill, including fermentation of most of its beer in closed tanks. However, brewers pump wort for the *Andechs Weissbier Hefetrüb* 300 meters up the hill to be fermented in open vessels.

The crew made the decision to use Sierra Nevada's four open 100-barrel fermenters to produce *Kellerweis*. "Those aren't really set up for *weizen*," Jennings explained. They have flat bottoms, like open fermenters in England, and lack a trough for skimming like in Germany.

Although what comes out of those fermenters accounts for the tiniest bit of what Sierra Nevada sells, they are constantly in use, fermenting batches of all styles that might be blended into a full run and, most notably, *Bigfoot Barleywine Style Ale* once a year.

The mash for *Kellerweis* includes one step—it is milled in at 155° F (68° C), then at mash full raised to 161° F (72° C). Fermentation takes place at 70° F (21° C), and at high kraeusen the froth regularly peaks above 4 feet and flows over the edges of the open tanks. Jennings calls the process continual kraeusening, because brewers fill the first of the four fermenters with yeast from Sierra Nevada's propagator, then use a portion of beer at high fermentation to dose each of the other three tanks.

He's happy with *Kellerweis,* but not necessarily with the yeast handling or the way the beer is moved around. "We tend to pursue things full gun and do what it takes to achieve the goal," he said. "Who knows where this will go? You might talk to me in a year and everything will have changed."

They experimented with using *speise* in the pilot brewery but it wasn't realistic on a production basis. "We tried bottle conditioning in every way it is done. It's nice to see what effects all these other methods have on your beer so you are able to make the final decision based on what you can do," Jennings said.

Using the open fermenters changed the ester profile of *Kellerweis* as well as other yeast-generated aromas and flavors. "We tended to be quite heavy on the phenolic notes. The yeast tends to be very good at 4-vinyl guaiacol," Jennings said. "Without changing our mashing schedule the yeast was more estery and less phenolic in the open fermenters."

The yeast also looks distinctive in the bottle.

"I've been answering emails all week saying there's a lot of gunk in the beer," Manley said a few months after *Kellerweis* hit the market. "Asking if there is snot."

Making Adjustments in New Jersey

Greg Zaccardi understands when he tastes something different. He understood it when he was first introduced to *weizen* beers while touring Bavaria with his wife, Simone. "I tasted the *hefe* and I said, 'Wow, there's nothing like this in the United States.' " And he understands it today when he drinks a *weizen* made with a decoction mash next to one brewed using a single-infusion mash.

Touring High Point Brewing in Butler, New Jersey, is not quite like visiting a comparably small brewery in Germany but it is as educational. High Point operates in part of what was the American Hard Rubber Mill, a sprawling historic building where the brewery shares space with a dozen different businesses. The 15-barrel Criveller system was designed to brew English-style ales. Although High Point initially used converted dairy tanks as fermenters, those were replaced with closed conicals.

When Zaccardi began selling the Ramstein brand beers in 1996, High Point was the first, and only, all-wheat brewery in the United States since before Prohibition, when *weissbier* breweries were tiny and made something that tasted more like wheat beers from Berlin. He since has begun brewing a variety of barley beers under contract, accounting for more than one-third of production. "We couldn't survive brewing wheat beer alone," he said.

"The biggest consumers of wheat beers want German wheat beers," he said. When he conducts blind tastings, which he calls the "Ramstein Challenge," locals like those at the Deutscher Club in a nearby town prefer his beers to well-known German *weiss* beers. "You can taste the difference in a locally brewed wheat beer," he said. "They love our beer, but it's not German. They still buy the German beers."

He uses primarily German malts. "I've always tried to support the local products, but you can't find the red wheat, for instance. I've looked close to home, and there's no good substitute," he said. "I'm not saying there's not a low-cost substitute. There's no substitute." He puts a premium on consistency. "One thing I learned from the brewmaster in Germany is your beer can always be excellent or always be bad. It can't go from excellent to bad to excellent. People will drink what they are used to."

He adapted his methods to make the Criveller system decoction friendly. He starts the mash in the boiling kettle, then transfers 75 percent of it to the lauter tun. "That's better because it isolates the thickest part of the mash," he said. He then boils that portion for 30 minutes. The first time he made his strong *Winter Wheat* he did three decoctions, and that turned into a 24-hour project. These days he sticks to a double-decoction beer.

In 2004 an agitator box broke and he could only do an infusion mash. "A lot of people will say decoction is a myth, but I can taste it. The depth of the malt taste. The middle notes are caramelly, sweet," he said. He's aware of the brewing studies that show that modern modified malts eliminate the need for decoction. "I've read the debate in *Brauwelt* (a German trade magazine). If it didn't make a difference I would do it. Especially with the cost of natural gas."

Before opening High Point he worked briefly at Edelweissbrauerei, a wheat beer brewery in Durren, Germany. There lagers fermented in open tanks, wheat beers in closed unitanks. Nonetheless, he set out to use open fermentation at High Point. "You can't achieve the consistency," he said. "You have to have a room that is clean enough to manufacture CDs. Otherwise you've got a six-week shelf life. Now we have a much more stable product."

Because his yeast—originally from Germany, now kept in a yeast bank—does not flocculate uniformly, he had to devise a way to effectively harvest yeast from the conical. "Some drops to the bottom, some hangs in the middle, and some is top fermenting," he said. Were he to draw off only from the bottom he would lose the banana and clove character in beers fermented with subsequent generations. He uses the racking arm in the fermenter to help keep yeast in suspension.

RAMSTEIN CLASSIC
Original Gravity: 1.054 (13.5 °P)
Alcohol by Volume: 5.4%
Apparent Degree of Attenuation: 78%
IBU: 12.5
Malts: Wheat, Pilsener, Munich, chocolate
Hops: Hallertau, Perle
Yeast: House yeast, acquired from Germany
Primary Fermentation: Yeast pitched at 60 to 70° F (16 to 21° C) depending on season, rises to 70 to 71° F (21 to 22° C), 5 days
Secondary Fermentation: 30 to 32° F (-1 to 0° C), 14 to 15 days
Also Noteworthy: Bottle conditioned

He seldom pushes a yeast beyond seven generations before propagating a new batch. "They say the second generation is the sweet spot. We try to get as close to that as we can," he said. "It does make a difference.

I can tell you in the last year when we went to ten (generations) we saw it. I guarantee it loses its ester and its phenolic profile."

He paused, thinking of another way to describe the result. "It becomes a lot more, I hate to say this, American," he said. Then he laughed.

He puts the yeast to work at about 60° F (16° C), although in warmer weather it will start higher, and lets it rise to 70 or 71° F (21 to 22° C). He used to hold the temperatures a little lower to promote cloviness, at the time saying, "There are a lot of banana wheat beers. Why would we try to copy, say, Weihenstephan?"

Ramstein Blonde, a pale *hefeweizen*, sells best, followed by the *Ramstein Classic*, initially called *Ramstein Dark*. Both have more banana character than early batches and now receive better reviews from the online beer community. "I've begun to appreciate the complexity that banana brings," Zaccardi said.

He originally aimed for 3.5 volumes of CO_2 in packaging, but bars couldn't properly dispense the beers on tap, so in 1998 Zaccardi lowered the target to 2.5 to 2.75 volumes. He calculates his *speise* addition so that it contributes 1.25 volumes on top of 1.5 naturally in the beer. High Point shoots for 20 days from opening a grain bag, the start of the production process, to tapping a keg.

Now that he has made a variety of styles under contract, such as a Belgian-style *dubbel* and a German-style Pilsener, Zaccardi remains convinced wheat beers present the greatest challenge for a brewer. "Brewing consistent wheat beer is the hardest thing to do," he said. "You have to control something that is uncontrollable, the yeast.

Don't Be Nice to Weiss

Jonathan Cutler takes a different approach to dealing with *weizen* yeast at Piece Brewery & Pizzeria in Chicago. He abuses it. "The thing a lot of people do is they brew it and they baby it," he said. "They give it oxygen, they treat it really nice. *Weiss* doesn't like that."

"I treat it like a redheaded stepchild. Kick the tank, underoxygenate it, anything nasty I can think of," he said, seriously without being too serious. Cutler's *weizen* beers, both *Top Heavy Hefeweizen* and *Dark-n-Curvy Dunkelweizen* regularly win medals in competitions such as the Great American Beer Festival and the World Beer Cup. So do other brewpub beers, although they would seem to be at a disadvantage since neither their brew houses nor fermentation areas mimic classic German design, nor can they dispense *weizen* beers with as much carbon dioxide as bottled versions. (Cutler does not bottle condition his beers for competitions, in case you wondered.)

Cutler doesn't repitch his yeast, always starting with a fresh batch. "I found this through trial and error, but I was glad to hear about Schneider (page 83)," he said. He thinks that means he is effectively underpitching, although he does not count yeast cells to know for sure. "I figure I am going in low and I don't oxygenate," he said. "You need to remember that yeast *wants* sugar."

His recipe for *Dark-n-Curvy* includes 60 percent wheat, a combination of light and dark. He's able to do a single-step infusion by starting very dry for the protein rest, in the 118 to 122° F (48 to 50° C) range. Lautering takes a little longer, up to 2½ hours compared to 1½ for other beers. "Our hope is the protein rest breaks things up a little," he said. He'll cut an "X" in the mash and has had to rouse it and stir to get it to lauter evenly.

Primary fermentation takes only 3 or 4 days in the mid-70s (22-24° C) and he'll let the beer sit warm for another 3 to 4 days before crashing to serving temperature. The quicker, the fresher the pub serves it, the better.

■■■ Speising It Up

Until recently packaging *hefeweizens* meant bottling. For instance, Weissbierbrauerei Schneider & Sohn did not start kegging its beer until 1993.

Although larger breweries now tank condition their beer, centrifuge it, and pasteurize it before packaging, German brewers have traditionally bottled *weissbier* with *speise*, and many still do. In *German Wheat Beer*, Eric Warner provides a complete overview of the variety of ways commercial brewers use *speise* or otherwise package their beers. This comes pretty naturally for homebrewers who already bottle condition beer, while pub brewers are limited by their draft systems and can only boost the CO_2 to as high a level as works.

Likewise, packaging breweries in the United States are sometimes limited by equipment, both the draft systems in establishments that sell draft beers and in bottling. For instance, Sierra Nevada aims for 2.55 to 2.65 volumes of CO_2 in kegs and 2.7 to 2.8 in bottles. High Point Brewing initially targeted 3.5 volumes but quickly lowered that to 2.75 volumes.

However, the beer will look and taste better at the levels of carbonation German brewers achieve, such as the 3.5 volumes (7 grams/liter) in *Schneider Weisse Original* or 3.6 in

Schlenkerla Rauchweizen. That can be accomplished using *speise* or sugar. "Sugar is clean. Wort is a complex thing in its own right," said New Glarus brewmaster Dan Carey. "*Speise* obviously works. It works great. What we use is based on what we've learned." He bottles both *Dancing Man Wheat* and *Crack'd Wheat* with about 2 million viable cells per milliliter and sugar, targeting 3.6 volumes of CO_2.

Eric Toft at Schönram figures using *speise* is worth the extra effort. Watching Bernard Kuhn at Weissbräu Freilassing helped him design a system that works for his relatively small output. Kuhn's approach is simpler still. He collects the first runnings from a batch brewed about five days in advance of when he will bottle. He puts the wort in a keg, inserts a steam coil, heats it to sterilize the wort, then lets the proteins created in the process settle out. "It makes a smoother flavor," he said.

Toft built a larger tank with a steam coil inside, making it easy to attach a hose. About five days before bottling *Festweisse* he collects the first runnings off his *helles* (the beer he brews most often) in the tank and heats it while recirculating the wort. He holds it for 20 minutes at 194° F (90° C), then shuts off the steam. He caps it with a sterile breather filter to allow air in as the wort cools. "The reason I do it this way is that this is seldom done, as it is too time-consuming," he said. "I wanted to set us apart from other breweries."

He gives *Festweisse* four months' shelf life. "Tastewise, that's the outside," he said. "In terms of turbidity we could probably go six to eight months." When I visited the brewery we opened a bottle that was just beyond four months. Although it had lost some of its brightest flavors, it still had a fresh taste seldom found in the United States. We let the glass sit for several hours in the *schalander* (the brewers' break room, complete with taps), and when we returned it was as cloudy as when we left.

In his book Warner provides the formula to calculate the amount of *speise* that needs to be added. The key numbers: target level of carbonation, the gravity of the young beer, and the starting and final gravities of the *speise*. The formula is a little complicated, so the numbers are presented only in grams and liters. A key, quick conversion to remember is that 2 grams per liter of CO_2 equals 1 volume. Beer at atmospheric pressure contains about 0.2 percent (2 grams/liter) of CO_2 at 60° F (16° C) and 1 gram of fermentable extract yields 0.46 grams of CO_2. A target of 3.5 volumes (0.7 percent) would require adding 1.08 grams extract to the beer; a target of 4 volumes (0.8 percent) would need 1.3 grams. The formula for the amount of *speise* that needs to be added to the young beer:

$$\% \text{ speise} = \frac{\frac{\% \text{ desired } CO_2 \text{ content} - 0.2}{0.46}}{\text{starting gravity-real final gravity (°Plato)}} \times 100$$

You must know the real (as opposed to the apparent) final gravity of the *speise* wort, which can be determined by multiplying the apparent terminal limit by 0.81. If you set aside *speise* from the original wort, you can start with the apparent terminal of the young beer.

chapter eight
A RECIPE FOR HEFEWEIZEN

"A lot of people will say decoction is a myth, but I can taste it."
– Greg Zaccardi, High Point Brewing

Bill Aimonetti checked the recipe again, then again. Yes, he used an English pale ale malt to brew *Haunta Weizen* when it won a wallful of homebrewing awards. In retrospect it makes perfect sense, because this was his basic base pale malt in the 1990s . . . and it worked. No doubt the devil is in the details when brewing *hefeweizen* beers, but not every single one of the details need be the same.

By the time he brewed a batch in 1997 that won the American Homebrewers Association Club-Only competition, Aimonetti, who lives in the mountains east of Albuquerque, had made the beer more than a half dozen times, including a couple in which he skipped decoction. "I didn't like the results," he said. "This is the only beer I feel I have to decoct." He notices more banana and clove, but more importantly a "malt softness" that sets the best *hefeweizens* apart.

Haunta Weizen won medals at multiple competitions—in successive years at Dixie Cup, at the Bluebonnet in Dallas, in the St. Louis Happy Holiday judging, in the Masters Championship of Amateur Brewing, and of course, in New Mexico. This recipe has been around the block,

Bill Aimonetti and his brewing system. (Photo courtesy of Bill Aimonetti.)

which is why I asked Bill if I could include it here. I happen to know about its success because he and I are friends, occasionally seeing each other at meetings of the Dukes of Ale (Albuquerque's homebrewing club), but more often drinking together, discussing flavor and process to a degree of detail not everybody enjoys as much as we do.

While looking over this recipe we were drinking somebody else's Belgian-style *wit*, in this case fermented with a Trappist yeast. We kept coming back to the fact the beer tasted so much of cloves (technically "4-vinyl guaiacol"). It reminded us that although the grist composition and production of ferulic acid set the table, the yeast strain and handling of fermentation determine the ultimate flavor of a *hefeweizen*.

Those merit a closer look before we get to the recipe itself.

Experiments in 2003 illustrated the strength of links between some Belgian yeast strains and wheat strains. "These are very plastic yeasts," said David Bryant of the Brewing-Science Institute (BSI) in Colorado, who conducted the study along with Larry Nielsen of Microanalytics and Dave Logsdon. "There are some yeasts, like Chico (the American ale yeast from Sierra Nevada Brewing), that you make a change in temperature or pitching rates and the beer still comes out the same. With (*weizen*) yeasts, you change anything just a little, and you get a different profile."

The study tested a variety of wheat and Belgian yeast strains—the Belgian strains primarily associated with Trappist and abbey-style beers—with a gas chromatograph, measuring the extent and concentration of various aroma compounds produced by different yeast strains in what might be called a "basic" wheat beer with about 14 IBU (Saaz hops). Malted and unmalted wheat made up 42 percent of the grist of the 1.058 (14.3 °P) base beer. The mash started at 122° F (50° C) for 30 minutes (a protein rest, but skipping the 113° F/45° C rest most agree is important for freeing ferulic acid), spent 30 minutes at 144° F (62° C), 30 more at 152° F (67° C), and 20 minutes at 155° F (68° C) before being raised to 170° F (77° C) for the sparge. Fermentation took place at 68° F to 70° F (20-21° C), and all beer reached a terminal gravity of 1.010 to 1.013 (2.5-3 °P).

Several Belgian yeasts registered significantly higher levels of 4-vinyl guaiacol than German and Bavarian wheat yeasts or the Belgian wheat yeasts. The panel identified them as spicy and singled out the clove in some cases. However, the panel also found the German wheat and Belgian *wit* strains produced significant levels of styrene—the resiny, hard plastic flavor described by some as phenolic—suggesting a metabolic link between styrene and 4-vinyl guaiacol. The wheat beer strains (particularly the one known as Weihenstephan 68) recorded high levels of isoamyl acetate, the esters responsible for banana and other fruit flavors and aromas. The results also indicated a correlation between styrene and phenyl ethyl alcohol, a rose-aroma necessary for the recognized aroma of beer.

"The *weizen* and *wit* yeasts tend to be more balanced, but you really can't lump any of them together," Bryant said. "Each one is a little different. Like people."

Brewers experienced with mostly lager yeasts and less-plastic ale yeast need to remember that thought when considering the variables involved in fermenting *weizen* beers. For more about ester production in all beers, Volume 2 of the *MBAA Practical Handbook for the Specialty Brewer* acts as an excellent primer.

Meanwhile, here is the short course on working with *weizen* yeast strains.

Yeast Selection and Cropping

As in *Brew Like a Monk*, White Labs and Wyeast, the largest yeast suppliers for the craft brewing and homebrewing communities, provided tables (see the Appendix) that include not only the information you usually see about their yeast (such as possible attenuation) but also flavor characteristics they expect those strains to produce with standard pitching rates and oxygenation levels.

However, unlike in *Brew Like a Monk* I did not ask them to list the sources of those strains. Some are well known, such as that WLP300 and Wyeast 3068 are variations on Weihenstephan 68, used by many Bavarian breweries. Or that Wyeast 3984 and WLP400 came originally from Hoegaarden. I'd rather that you consider the profiles as a guide—or if you follow a similar path when using other strains, such as from BSI[1]— because they are not the exact same strains and will not produce the same flavors in vessels of different sizes, at different temperatures, interacting with worts with different levels of ferulic acid, and . . . it's a long list.

Outside of the largest brewing companies in Bavaria, brewers commonly exchange yeasts. "You can't tell me the guys in the north use (Weihenstephan) 68," Bryant said, referring to breweries closer to the area where the Degenberg family first popularized *weizen* beer than to Munich. "Those beers are spicy, phenol heavy. Even more than *Schneider*."

Strains are bound to change, sometimes from one generation to the next. "One mistake Americans make is to bottom crop *hefe* (strains). You get a lot of strain drift that way," Bryant said. "The second and third generations, you get more phenols. Every time you crop you'll get a little more. That's particularly true with 68."

Scott Jennings of Sierra Nevada said that the brewery experimented with bottom cropping while developing the process for *Kellerweis*. "Bad, bad plan," he said.

---

[1] Culturing your own yeast from bottles of commercial examples may not work. Many larger German breweries bottle condition with a lager yeast after centrifuging or filtering out the primary yeast.

Bryant estimates that about 90 percent of his brewery customers—mostly brewpubs and small microbreweries—pitch fresh yeast. One client who uses yeast multiple times will brew two batches of *hefeweizen*, then use the yeast to make a batch of Belgian-style *wit*.

Smaller breweries in Germany pitch the same yeast for many generations. At Weissbräu Freilassing Bernard Kuhn picks up a new batch from a larger nearby brewery about every six months. At the Brauereigasthof Schneider owner-to-be Matthias Schneider said that his family has used the same yeast since 1989, wanting to maintain the house character, but refreshes it often. Like Greg Zaccardi in New Jersey he wonders if there is a "sweet spot."

"Yeast needs— how do you say it?—time to be strong. It's running better after the fourth or fifth generation," he said.

Fermentation Temperatures

Although *weizen* and *wit* yeasts obviously share much in common with Belgian ale yeasts, they are not as alcohol tolerant. The White Lab and Wyeast charts provide a guide to targeting fermentation temperatures. The practices of breweries with open fermenters indicate they may allow temperatures to drift higher because other factors may come into play. Basically, higher temperatures produce pleasant floral and fruity esters, but at the risk of creating unpleasant solvency notes (ethyl acetate). Additionally, lower levels of esters promote the perception of phenols.

Pitching Rates

German brewing literature suggests pitching 4 million to 7 million cells per milliliter in brewing a standard Bavarian *hefeweizen*. Weissbierbrauerei Schneider currently pitches 7 million in *Schneider Weisse Original*, a 12.8 °P beer, although brewmaster Hans-Peter Drexler and laboratory technicians were exploring a plan in the fall of 2009 to boost that rate.

"You've got to be careful when talking about pitching rates," said Dan Carey at New Glarus Brewing. "Are you talking about sending in 5 million little old ladies from a rest home or 5 million soldiers ready for battle? Until you calculate the vitality of the yeast, that number doesn't mean much."

Carey pitches 7 million cells per milliliter in *Dancing Man Wheat* (16 °P) and 5 million per milliliter in *Crack'd Wheat* (13.5 °P), however, he has a yeast propagator and knows he is putting particularly vital yeast to work. As does Schneider.

In fact, very high and very low pitching rates increase ester production. The danger of underpitching is creating higher rates of ethyl acetate, the solventy character best described as nail polish remover and a bad complement for clovy phenols in a *weizen*.

Fermenter Geometry

As with other brewing research, studies involving fermenter geometry have focused on lager beers. Ester production by yeast is inversely related to yeast growth, but research by Greg Casey at Coors has shown this relationship can be uncoupled by fermenter design. Casey presented his findings at the 2005 Rocky Mountain Microbrewing Symposium. In simplest terms, when CO_2 levels increase around the yeast in a fermenter, the levels of ester production decrease. For instance, when some breweries replaced box fermenters with cylindroconicals they found the greater height-to-width ratio reduced ester character. The change was more pronounced in taller, "skinnier" fermenters—something homebrewers using Cornelius kegs as fermenters might want to remember, likewise those making decisions at commercial breweries while trying to maximize fermentation volume in limited floor space.

Fermenter Configuration Influences on Ester and Phenol Production

	Isoamyl acetate mg/l	Vinyl guaiacol mg/l
Open vessel	5.1	2.5
Horizontal tank	3.7	2.4
Vertical tank	3.5	1.6
Cylindro-conical tank (CCT)	2.3	1.7

Source: Ausgewählte Kapitel der Brauereitechnologie

Research in Germany has found that levels of both 4-vinyl guaiacol and isoamyl acetate increase substantially in open fermenters. Further anecdotal evidence, from scores of breweries across Bavaria to Sierra Nevada Brewing back in the United States, indicate that open fermentation produces a balance of esters and phenols *weizen* beers are recognized for. Further studies at Weissbierbraurei Schneider indicate that contact with oxygen during open fermentation promotes production of 4-vinyl guaiacol, a reason breweries using closed fermenters may choose to increase aeration.

Open fermenters also make skimming what the Germans call *brandhefe*, the bitter-tasting dead yeast and cold break that surges to the top during fermentation, possible.

Although Sierra Nevada Brewing has gone to particular lengths in order to use open fermentation for its *Kellerweis*, most commercial breweries must make do with their closed fermenters. Brewmaster Jonathan Cutler briefly considered taking the lid off a Grundy tank at Piece Brewery & Pizzeria in Chicago, but, he said, "we've got pizza yeast in the air everywhere."

When Aimonetti first brewed *Haunta Weizen*, he most often conducted fermentation in glass carboys (he since has built stainless steel fermenters and experimented with open fermentation). Because the *weizen* fermentation was so robust, he used plastic buckets and left the lid loose. "In a way I was using open fermentation without thinking about it," he said.

He wrote this recipe after reading *German Wheat Beer*, drawing directly from Eric Warner's book in formulating his decoction mash. Reading scoresheets from homebrewing competitions he quickly saw clove character made *Haunta Weizen* stand out. One judge even accused him of putting cloves in his beer.

Original Gravity: 1.055
Final Gravity: 1.012
Alcohol by Volume: 4.9%
IBU: 15

Grain Bill:
Pale ale malt (Hugh Baird) 36.4%
Wheat malt (Weyermann) 63.6%

Mashing:
Begin mashing at 105° F (41° C), then raise to 112° F (50° C) for 25 minutes. Pull a 40% decoction, heat that to 160° F (71° C) for 15 minutes, then bring it to boiling for 20 minutes. Re-combine the decoction at 147° F (64° C) for 20 minutes. Raise to 160° F (71° C) for 30 minutes, then to 170° F (77° C) for mash-out. Do not aerate wort during decoction.

Hops:
Czech Saaz, 90 minutes (7.9 IBU)
Czech Saaz, 60 minutes (6.5 IBU)
Czech Saaz, 15 minutes (1.6 IBU)
Boil: 90 minutes
Yeast: Wyeast 3068 Weihenstephan Weizen, pitched from 1-gallon starter
Fermentation: 7 days at 63° F (17° C), 7 days at 68° F (20° C)
Bottling: Primed with 1 gallon of wort saved in refrigerator

When Bill brews a wheat beer these days, it is more likely to be a *wit* (he might have been happier to provide that recipe, which has also won a few awards). "I prefer the occasional citrus. The citrus, rather than banana and clove. It's more refreshing," he said. "Once I went to Celis (when the brewery was still operating in Austin, Texas) I knew *hefe* was doomed."

PART IV:
THE WHEAT BEERS OF AMERICA

chapter nine
A HEFEWEIZEN BY ANY OTHER NAME...

"I'm not sure this could have happened anywhere else in 1985. The people in the Northwest are the grandsons and granddaughters of pioneers. They are willing to try anything."
– Kurt Widmer, Widmer Brothers Brewing

The bartender appeared skeptical, and when the guy pouring the beer has his doubts then don't bet on that beer. It was the spring of 1996 in Milwaukee, and Kegel's Inn on West National Avenue had recently begun selling this newfangled beer from Oregon called *Widmer Hefeweizen* beside several traditional German-made *weissbiers*.

Kegel's was a throwback even then, old-fashioned, with an antique bar, stained-glass windows depicting drinking scenes, hunting murals, and a German-focused menu—except on Friday, when the Wisconsin-style fish fry is one of the best in town. It has changed little since 1996, these days still offering several German *weissbiers* on tap.

"The distributor says this is going to sell better than sliced bread," the bartender said. The beer would be brewed at the former Val Blatz brewery on Tenth Street. He looked at the tap handles again. The look on his face made it clear he wasn't a believer. "People here know what *hefeweizen* is."

Beer enthusiasts who hate that Widmer Brothers Brewing calls its beer "*hefeweizen*" love this story. They figure that the plan for Milwaukee did not work out—the Widmers decided not to exercise their option on the Blatz facility, and these days you won't find *Widmer Hefeweizen* on tap at Kegel's—because the brothers should have called their unfiltered wheat beer anything else. That's not the lesson the Widmers learned. "It was the first time we realized the way we brew beer wouldn't work everywhere," Rob Widmer said. The Milwaukee brewery was designed to crank out light lagers using decoction mashing and adjuncts, and never produced beers the Widmers were happy with.

That didn't prove to be a setback. The Widmers expanded many times over, sold a portion of the company to Anheuser-Busch (now AB InBev), bought a share of Goose Island Beer Company, and merged with Redhook Ale Brewery. In 1985 they brewed the beer themselves in the morning, then in the afternoon loaded beer into a used 1970 Datsun pickup truck they had bought from their father, Ray. Now they run the eleventh-largest brewery in the country. The cloudy wheat beer the brothers started selling in 1986 continues to account for 60 percent of production in the state-of-the-art brew house the Widmers installed in 1996.

Meanwhile, "American Hefeweizen" and "American Wheat" emerged as styles according to the Brewers Association, which organizes the Great American Beer Festival and World Beer Cup competitions. Still other beers brewed with a significant portion of wheat have grown to be among the best sellers for many of the country's fastest-growing breweries. Quite a change in a land that had little wheat beer tradition before the 1980s.

Scores of American breweries made *weiss* beers, sometimes called "Berliner Weiss" and in that style no matter the name, during the nineteenth century. That should be no surprise, given the wave of German emigration beginning in the 1840s, including both beer drinkers and the brewers who would make their beer. About that time the popularity of southern German *weizen* was near its low, and Berliner *weisse* was the toast of the north.

Few American *weiss* breweries produced significant amounts of beer, but they made a lasting impression because they bottled everything, leaving plenty of evidence behind. Because *weiss* beer was low in

Weissbierbrauerei Schneider brewmaster Hans-Peter Drexler (above) in the brewery's fermentation room. Below, Georg Schneider's 1862 recipe for weissbier sits under glass in a mini-museum at the brewery.

Scott Jennings skims billowing yeast from open fermenters at Sierra Nevada Brewing in California. (Photo courtesy of Sierra Nevada.)

Scott Smith shovels grain from his mash tun at East End Brewing in Pittsburgh. (Photo courtesy of Scott Smith.)

As in Germany, open fermenters at New Glarus Brewing (above) have self-skimming chutes. These make dealing with runoff easier than at Sierra Nevada. New Glarus brewmaster Dan Carey (below) on a sunny day in front of the new hilltop brewery. (Top photo courtesy of New Glarus Brewing.)

Brewmaster Bernard Kuhn (above) sanitizes bottles at Weissbräu Freilassing. The wheat-beer-only brewery is the last in Germany to use wood-fired kettles (below).

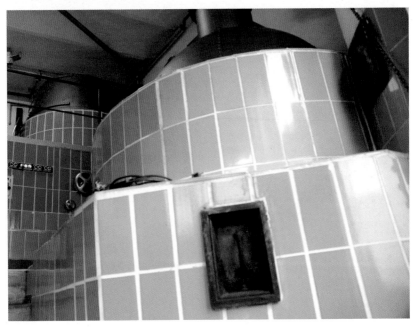

Open fermenters at Private Landbrauerei Schönram (above) in the south of Germany. They can be closed easily for cleaning. Brewmaster Eric Toft, originally from Wyoming, has a view of the Alps from his office window (below).

Matthias Richter (above) stands beside one of his copper vessels at Bayerischer Bahnhof Gasthaus and Gose Brauerei in Leipzig. Below, a glass holds Döllnitzer Ritterguts Gose at the bistro Sinfonie in Leipzig.

Head brewer Jason Perkins (left) and founder Rob Tod monitor the transfer of a special mash at Allagash Brewing. (Photo courtesy of Allagash Brewing.)

Boulevard Unfiltered Wheat *shows up at places where special beers have not previously been available, such as in aluminum bottles on ice in the snack area at Mount Rushmore National Memorial in South Dakota.*

Rob (left) and Kurt Widmer (with the level) and their father, Ray, in 1984 in the original Widmer Brothers brewery. Below, Kurt (left) and Rob in 2009 in their state-of-the-art brew house. (Photos courtesy of Widmer Brothers Brewing.)

alcohol, it could be sold on Sunday in places where lager was banned. In Brooklyn, for instance, nine of thirty-five breweries bottled beer in 1884, and eight of those were small *weiss* breweries. At least twenty-five *weiss* beer breweries operated in Philadelphia during the second half of the century, but they produced only 4,125 barrels in 1879 and 8,750 barrels in 1890. That amounted to about one-half of 1 percent of the city's beer production. [1]

In 1882 *The Western Brewer*, a trade publication, described *weiss* beer as the lightest beer made, being yellowish in color, tickling "the tongue on account of the large amount of carbonic acid it contains." It had a slightly sour or acid wine taste and was very quenching but would not keep fresh longer than about a week in summer were a great quantity of hops not added. The journal offered details about production: "While the beer is fermenting (which is about twenty-four hours from the time of preparation) it has to be filled into bottles, or else it not only loses in strength, but will become sour. When the beer is filled into bottles, it contains a trifle of alcoholic substance, but it is not yet beer, and first becomes drinkable after being filled into the bottles and undergoing the proper time of fermentation therein. After twenty hours it is drinkable, though more perfect in forty-eight hours." [2]

Eighteen years later another report in *The Western Brewer* stated: "The *weiss* beer made in the United States is generally made by the same methods of mashing and fermentation as in Berlin, top fermentation, with the peculiar Berlin *weisse* beer yeast being essential, the same as a fair percentage of wheat malt used in connection with barley malt. Most of the American *weiss* beers made in this fashion are essentially identical with the genuine Berlin article, and do not differ much from this or among themselves any more than *weiss* beers of different makers in Berlin differ from one another. Besides the *weiss* beer made in the manner stated there is frequently another *weiss* beer made which we believe is generally sold as *weiss* beer, pure and simple, and not distinguished by the appellation of Berlin *weisse* beer, and sells at a somewhat lower price, we are informed. This kind of *weiss* beer is made of a wort made similar to an ordinary

[1] Rich Wagner, "Philadelphia Weiss Beer Brewers," *American Breweriana Journal* 159 (May-June 2009): 9.

[2] "What Weiss Beer Is," *The Western Brewer: and Journal of the Barley, Malt, and Hop Trades* (March 15, 1882): 889.

lager beer wort, somewhat thinner, however, and with a liberal percentage of raw grain and rather complete saccharification."[3]

However, the *American Handy Book of the Brewing, Malting, and Auxiliary Trades* offered a different view in 1902: "The material employed and the manner of mashing is much different. Wheat malt is sometimes but not generally used. Instead, grits are employed to the amount of about 30 percent, together with pale malt." The wort was boiled for only 30 minutes. This resulted in a very different beer.

"Undoubtedly the American article could be much improved upon by employing the materials, as well as the mashing method in vogue in German *weiss* breweries, especially the material, as grits will under no circumstance yield those albuminoids that give *weiss* beer its character, as wheat malt does. Certainly there seems no reason why American *weiss* beer brewers should not be able to procure a good wheat malt.

"*Weiss* beer in America is sometimes stored, bunged, and fined like lager beer, but a brilliant *weiss* beer does not seem to catch the fancy of consumers, who are accustomed to the cloudy, lively article of Berlin fame."[4]

The experience of the Beltz Brewing Company in Cleveland seems typical. A native of Germany's Rhine Valley, Joseph Beltz immigrated to America in 1867, first working for a lager brewery. He set up his own business as a cooper, then added a saloon and wine shop in the same location. By 1876 he was brewing *weiss* beer. His was the smallest brewery in Cleveland, producing 500 barrels in 1884. He retooled the brewery in 1898 to manufacture ale and porter, then introduced lager beer in 1901. The company sold 10,000 barrels that year, and production grew to 75,000 in 1906.

The brewery quit making *weiss* beer altogether in 1905, although one of Beltz's offspring, Carl, started his own *weiss* beer brewery, operating it until 1914. Over the years a handful of other *weiss* beer breweries came and went in Cleveland, but by the time Prohibition began in 1919 all had closed.[5]

---

[3] "Different Weiss Beers," *The Western Brewer: and Journal of the Barley, Malt, and Hop Trades* (July 15, 1900): 282.

[4] Robert Wahl and Max Henius, *American Handy Book of the Brewing, Malting, and Auxiliary Trades* (Chicago: Wahl & Henius, 1901), 817.

[5] Carl Miller, *Breweries of Cleveland* (Cleveland: Schnitzelbank Press, 1998), 38-39.

The original Widmer Brothers brewery, circa 1985. (Photo courtesy of Widmer Brothers.)

Anchor Brewing in San Francisco created America's first post-Prohibition wheat beer, releasing *Anchor Wheat* in 1983. The beer contained 60 percent malt and was filtered, but most importantly, it was fermented with Anchor's ale yeast. Other breweries and brewpubs—remember, there weren't many of either—followed the example, using neutral ale yeast to brew with wheat rather than distinctive German *weizen* yeast or Belgian *wit* yeast.

Even Miller Brewing noticed, test marketing a wheat ale called *Dakota* in 1986. The late Jim Robertson, author of many tasting logs, called it a very good beer. "You could drink a lot of it. Very satisfying," he said. "It was an American wheat beer, not cloves or bananas, but it went down smooth." *Dakota* flunked its test, causing beer expert Michael Jackson to suggest Miller could have selected "more sophisticated" markets.

Perhaps Miller should have considered Portland, Oregon. There, brothers Kurt and Rob Widmer brewed just one beer when they opened for business in 1984, an assertive *alt* fermented with a yeast strain acquired from Germany. They weren't looking for the next new thing when they made *Widmer Weizen* their second beer, instead something light to complement *Widmer Altbier*.

Like other small brewers in the 1980s the Widmers didn't want to introduce a second yeast strain into their brewery, so they used their *alt* yeast to ferment the wheat beer and filtered it. "If our beer was a little cloudy people thought there was something wrong," Rob Widmer said, and because the Widmers' filter was rudimentary they got phone calls. "People would complain and we'd ask what it tasted like," Rob said. The customers weren't about to find out. "They'd say, 'We're not going to drink it. It's gone off.' "

Carl Simpson at the Dublin Pub, one of Portland's original beer outposts, called with a different sort of request. He wanted a third Widmer beer to sell, one he could sell "cask-conditioned." "He would lie to us and tell us everything was selling, but in truth the *alt* wasn't," Kurt Widmer said. (Avid beer fans loved *Widmer Altbier,* but it wasn't until a friend at the Henry Weinhard Brewery had it analyzed that the Widmers learned it contained more than 60 bitterness units.) The brothers couldn't brew a third beer because they only had two fermenters, but they did offer to let Simpson sell unfiltered wheat beer as a Dublin Pub brand.

"Carl took the time to explain the cloudiness to people," Rob said. The pub served the beer in a 23-ounce glass garnished with a lemon, and Simpson would have his waitstaff load a tray with glasses and walk through the pub. Naturally, other customers would ask about what was on the tray and usually end up ordering the same.

The Dublin stayed open until 2 a.m., becoming a gathering spot for waitstaff from places that shut down at 1 a.m., and soon other pubs were calling to ask for unfiltered wheat beer. "We (still) had serious reservations," Kurt said. "The clever Widmer brothers tried to talk them out of this."

"In retrospect I'm sure our yeast counts were all over the place," Rob said. His brother added that yeast could be so thick it looked like a glass of milk. Nobody was sending back cloudy beers anymore. "Bartenders would tap a keg and save the first pours for themselves," Rob said.

They decided to call the unfiltered beer *Widmer Hefeweizen,* to indicate, as Germans do, that the beer is cloudy because it's served with yeast (*hefe* meaning yeast in German). "In 1986 we weren't thinking style. We were just brewing beer," Rob said. The brothers are justifiably sensitive after listening to complaints about the name for going on twenty-five years. "They are totally discounting that people liked the beer," Rob said.

"We were very careful to make the distinction," Kurt said. The name has served them well. "Out here there was no standard (for *hefeweizen*)," Rob said. To this day when he ventures away from Oregon some consumers refuse a free taste simply because the beer is cloudy, but even more because they know the southern German style and don't like it. "The clovy phenolic is a love-hate flavor. Only three or four people out of ten are going to like it, and most of the others will really hate it. Our beer is much more approachable," he said.

The cloudy beer with a distinctive Cascade kick (and 30 bitterness units) introduced more drinkers to craft beer in the region that calls itself "Beervana" than any other single beer. No surprise that Hart Brewing, which introduced *Pyramid Wheaten Ale* in 1985, would offer *Pyramid Hefeweizen*, and that others like Nor'Wester and Redhook followed. Still, Widmer was selling *Hefeweizen* as fast as the brewery could make it.

"In the beginning it was six days from grain to glass," Rob said. They sold their beer only on draft until 1996, when the new brew house came online. By then, making 68,000 barrels a year, Widmer became the largest draft-only brewery in the Western Hemisphere, something that was hard to give up. "We struggled with that," Kurt said. "To this day people equate draft beer with better quality."

WIDMER HEFEWEIZEN
Original Gravity: 1.047 (11.75 °P)
Alcohol by Volume: 4.9%
Apparent Degree of Attenuation: 78%
IBU: 30
Malts: Wheat, pale
Hops: Willamette, Cascade
Yeast: House *alt* yeast
Primary Fermentation: 68° F (20° C), 4 days
Secondary Fermentation: 41° F (5° C), at least 2 days
Also Noteworthy: Centrifuged before bottling

Widmer Hefeweizen starts with soft water from the Bull Run Watershed—the source of Portland city water since 1895—that the brewery hardens a bit before mashing with about an equal measure of malted wheat and barley. The brothers have used both hard red and soft white wheat, and the brewery's sensory evaluation panel can't tell the difference. The step-infusion mash starts at 120° F (49° C), with saccharification at 148° F (64° C), because that's the way they've always done it. "I just used a textbook," Kurt said. The brothers smile often as they trade stories about what they knew, and didn't know, during the first years of operation. "We learn so much every year. That's why it's still fun," Kurt said.

Initially they boiled wort for 90 minutes, but shortened that to 75 minutes after their sensory panel found no flavor difference. The 5-vessel brew house yields 250 barrels, and although unitanks used for fermentation hold 1,500 barrels they aren't jacketed to the top (so effectively hold 1,100 barrels of *hefeweizen*, 1,300 of other beers). Fermentation at 68° F (20° C) lasts 6 days, and beer can be ready to ship in 2 more if necessary. More often it sits 4 days after primary at 68° F (20° C), then 2 days at 41° F (5° C) before packaging.

Lightly centrifuged, *Widmer Hefeweizen* contains 2.3 volumes of CO_2 in the keg and bottles. Shelf life for draft beer is 60 days, for bottles 120 days.

In the seventh and last edition of his *Pocket Guide to Beer* Michael Jackson gave *Widmer Hefeweizen* three (out of four) stars, noting the heavy sediment, of course, and writing the beer "tastes somewhere between a beer and a fresh, sweetish grapefruit juice, but deserves points for that curious distinction."

For many drinkers it "defines the style," although neither the BJCP nor the Brewers Association necessarily agrees. "Our beer has isoamyl acetate (banana) at low levels," Rob said. "Judges will sometimes notice that and leave a note, something like 'nice beer, wrong style.' The guidelines are very specific that the American style does not have banana." Nonetheless, *Widmer Hefeweizen* medals more often at the Great American Beer Festival than it doesn't. In 2009 *Pyramid Hefeweizen* won gold and the Widmers took silver.

Those who witnessed *Widmer Hefeweizen's* impact in Oregon don't tend to focus on guidelines. Speaking in 1996, shortly before Widmer began bottling (and since has experienced fourfold growth), Jerome Chicvara, co-founder of Full Sail Brewing in nearby Mount Hood, said:

"I think that Kurt Widmer's American rendition of a German style pioneered an entirely new beer style in the United States. Everything else is a copy."

chapter ten

BREWING IN A MELTING POT

"There is a lot of tradition in Belgium, while there is a lot more experimentation going on here."

– Steven Pauwels, Boulevard Brewing

Dan Carey has been a sucker for copper kettles since he was a kid and saw them shimmering in the giant windows at the Olympia Brewery in Tumwater, Washington. This particular day he barely pauses at the four domes saved from a couple of defunct German breweries and installed here at New Glarus Brewing, because time's a wastin'.

"Let's go down below where the real brewing happens," he says.

At the top of the stairs he plants his hands on both sides of the railing, quickly lifting himself and swinging his legs forward, covering the first two steps in an instant. He's a boots-on guy, happiest out on the brewery floor. And the $21-million, state-of-the-art hilltop brewery he and his wife and partner, Deb, built in New Glarus, Wisconsin, is the perfect extension of his brewing philosophy.

It is automated where he thinks it should be. "The automation does not mean you push a button and walk away," he says. "I'd say it takes more talent and skill to operate an automated brewery." It's traditional when he thinks that is appropriate, so it has everything needed to produce beers with the classic flavors and aromas associated with southern

German *weizens*. Two open fermenters sit behind glass, much as at Ayinger, the German brewery where he once interned. There's space for a third. The fermenters are empty right now, but the spicy banana aroma coming from the yeast propagator in a nearby room indicates *Dancing Man Wheat* will be brewed tomorrow.

"It drove the Germans crazy when we told them we wanted to use 5 percent oats in a wheat beer," Carey says. Krones, a German company, made most of the equipment, and the conversation turns to the Reinheitsgebot, Germany's 1516 "beer purity" law. "That's like saying you only cook with pork." *Dancing Man* not only contains a portion of oats but also packs a bigger punch for a south German *hefeweizen*—7.2 percent alcohol by volume—than almost anybody's style guidelines call for.

"I'm not a category brewer," Carey says, eschewing the word "style."

In fact, he has brewed a Berliner *weisse* with 5 percent Pinot Grigio grape juice and 5 percent Riesling juice. He also has mixed the flavors and aromas of American hops and German *weizen* yeast in a beer called *Crack'd Wheat*, giving every beer judge and would-be judge the opportunity to write "not to style."

Midwestern farmers don't grow as much wheat as in the past, but the region still proudly considers itself America's "breadbasket," and its brewers have used wheat to create a variety of beers like none found in Michael Jackson's 1977 *World Guide to Beer*. In Michigan, where Bell's Brewery built its reputation on a range of bold beers, its very different *Oberon Ale* accounts for half of sales. In Kansas City seven out of ten beers Boulevard Brewing sells are made with wheat. *Sunset Wheat* is a top seller for Leinenkugel in Wisconsin and *312 Urban Wheat* likewise for Goose Island in Chicago.

Talking about his brewery's unfiltered wheat beer, John Bryan of Boulevard said, "The grain is a part of many Midwesterners' lives, especially Kansans, and there is a feeling of local support when you purchase it. Around here we sell *Unfiltered Wheat* in rural taverns, VFW halls, places where you would not expect to see craft beer as part of the lineup. People take pride in their history of wheat farming, and they show it when they buy a wheat beer."

Early settlers in southern Wisconsin apparently tried to raise wheat but found the soil more suited to raising cattle. Swiss immigrants who moved to New Glarus in 1845 (the town is still known as "Little Switzerland") instead established a cheesemaking tradition that continues today. About nine out of ten of the cows that graze in the pastures throughout Green County are Holsteins, the variety that inspired the name of New Glarus Brewing's flagship beer, *Spotted Cow*.

When the Careys founded New Glarus Brewing in 1993, Dan thought it would be fun to build a *weiss*-only brewery. "Of course, we'd have been out of business long ago," he said.

He might be wrong. After earning a degree in brewing science from the University of California at Davis, he worked three years at a microbrewery at Montana before serving an internship at the Ayinger Brewery southwest of Munich; was valedictorian of a thirteen-week Siebel Institute Course in Brewing Science and Technology; installed dozens of small breweries for equipment maker J.V. Northwest; and spent three years as brewing supervisor at Anheuser-Busch's Fort Collins, Colorado, plant. He also took and passed the Diploma Master Brewer Examination at the Institute of Brewing in London, becoming the first American in nineteen years to do so.

Few American brewers know more about the basics of brewing wheat beers with southern German *weizen* yeasts. Carey and Sierra Nevada Brewing co-founder Ken Grossman wrote the chapter on Fermentations and Cellar Operations in Volume 2 of the *MBAA Practical Handbook for the Specialty Brewer,* and Carey took charge of two succinct sections dealing with *hefeweizen.*

"We did a lot of experiments," Carey said, talking about the journey from the first wheat beer he brewed at New Glarus in 1993 to *Dancing Man Wheat* and *Crack'd Wheat.* He and his staff experimented with half a dozen yeast strains, compared red wheat to white, changed mashing regimens and fermentation schemes. "It became glaringly evident which one of each was good for us," he said. "For every brewery it will be different."

He refers to *Crack'd Wheat* as "the culmination of all I have learned about brewing and what is important to me." Early in 2008 he concocted *Imperial Weizen,* 9.6 percent alcohol by volume and finished with American hops, as part of New Glarus's Unplugged series, special one-time releases he brews about four times a year. He doesn't drink that many strong beers ("I'm kind of a wimp when it comes to high alcohol"), but this was one he sometimes would sit down and drink by itself, treating it like a nightcap.

NEW GLARUS CRACK'D WHEAT
Original Gravity: 1.053 (13.5 °P)
Alcohol by Volume: 6%
Apparent Degree of Attenuation: 86%
IBU: 36
Malts: Pilsener, wheat, caramel
Hops: Hallertau Tradition, Cascade, Amarillo
Yeast: *Weizen* yeast from Bavaria
Primary Fermentation: Proprietary
Secondary Fermentation: In the bottle

In the fall of 2008 he visited Abbaye d'Orval, one of Belgium's six Trappist monasteries with a brewery, on his way home from Germany. A conversation with brewmaster Jean-Marie Rock eventually inspired him to make *Crack'd Wheat*. "He said, 'I don't know why everybody wants to copy my beer. They should invent their own style.' So *Crack'd Wheat* is *my* beer."

Unlike in *Dancing Man* Carey doesn't use a decoction mash to brew it and doesn't include oats in the grist. Cascade and Amarillo hops on top of Hallertau Tradition, including a solid dose of dry hops, turn this into what would best be called "an American beer brewed with wheat." Like *Dancing Man* it becomes beer in open fermenters. Many small American brewers have turned dairy equipment into makeshift open fermenters, but at New Glarus they are purpose-built with self-skimming chutes like those in Germany.

Like Eric Toft at Private Landbrauerei Schönram, Carey wants to know about both the wheat and barley varieties in the malts he buys. "Not only variety but growing region affects flavor, haze stability, and foam stability," Carey said. "I think most brewers think about six-row versus two-row, summer versus winter, maltster versus maltster, U.S.-Canada versus Europe. (But) they take whatever variety is available. I ask my maltsters to include the barley variety mix in their analysis data. Having a malt analysis without varietal data is like describing a dog without knowing the breed."

When New Glarus opened, Deb Carey said, "We try to make everything exactly true to style. That's our niche." That has changed. "When we started out we tried to explore styles in a classic way," Dan Carey said. "Now we say, 'inspired' by them." He has taken ideas from every traditional brewing nation and, when asked, said he couldn't point to just one.

"I'm like the Japanese, or like the Australian winemaker," he said. "I try to learn from everybody and take what I can use."

Beer From America's Breadbasket

Boulevard Brewing's flagship wheat beer did not always pour like a hazy sunrise on a humid Missouri morning, and sure wasn't the beer now so popular in Midwestern upscale restaurants and small-town VFW halls alike. In the mid-1990s the Kansas City brewery even considered dropping the beer before giving it new life as Boulevard *Unfiltered Wheat Beer*. These days the brewery sells more *UWB* alone than most other craft breweries produce overall, about 90,000 31-gallon barrels in 2009.

Belgian-born and -trained brewmaster Steven Pauwels, who went to work at Boulevard in 1999, understands his responsibility. "We've worked on this for ten years, keeping particles in suspension," he said. Cloudy sells and, to repeat one of this book's underlying themes using a

In 1990 Boulevard sold Boulevard Wheat Beer in rather plain-looking 12-packs. In October 2009 a customer gave an unopened pack to the brewery, where it is now on display.

Midwestern phrase, haze stability is "tougher than a cob." However, he doesn't consider it his biggest challenge.

"It's got to be microbiology," he said, guiding me around one of two laboratories within the Boulevard brewery. "Low IBU. High protein. Bugs love it."

I learned some time ago that letting a brewer decide what to show you within a brewery tells you what he thinks is important, so it was interesting that while working on this book I often found myself getting a tour of brewery labs. In fact, when I visited Bell's Brewery in Michigan, quality control director Gary Nicholas gave me the entire tour. "It's really easy to have a clean brewery if you don't look," he said. "Microbiology is super important when you don't filter or pasteurize."

See a shared concern? Lactic (or "wild") flavors were once common in the white beers of Belgium, and some modern brewers may choose to explore them, including Boulevard with *Two Jokers Double Wit*. However, those characteristics are not part of the flavor profiles of Boulevard *Unfiltered Wheat*, Bell's *Oberon*, Harpoon *UFO Hefeweizen*, Three Floyds *Gumballhead*, or many other wheat beers brewed in the United States.

About ten years after beer drinkers in Portland, Oregon, would pause if served a cloudy glass of *Widmer Weizenbier*, the story was repeated in the Midwest. Simple chill haze nearly killed *Boulevard Wheat Beer* in the mid-1990s. "Some draft accounts had beers returned from the table because customers thought there was something wrong with it," recalled Bryan, director of the Artisanal Division at Boulevard. "We tried to explain that chill haze can't hurt you, but a few retailers would have none of it. They wanted clear beer, regardless. Then our top account for wheat, Harling's Upstairs, took us off tap over it."

Boulevard's leadership rightfully worried about the brewery's overall reputation and considered dropping the brand. Instead they returned to an earlier plan, to test selling the beer unfiltered, starting in the brewery tasting room bar. Not until Boulevard added a centrifuge was the beer bottled. Sales jumped after the Grand Street Café began serving *Unfiltered Wheat* with a lemon wedge. Like the Dublin Pub in Portland, the café was a place where other servers hung out and—this is starting to sound awfully familiar—the practice quickly spread across town.

BOULEVARD UNFILTERED WHEAT
Original Gravity: 1.045 (11.3 °P)
Alcohol by Volume: 4.4%
Apparent Degree of Attenuation: 75%
IBU: 13
Malts: Pale, wheat, unmalted wheat, Munich
Hops: Simcoe (varieties vary)
Yeast: House, English pale ale

Primary Fermentation: Yeast pitched at 64° F (18° C), rises to 73° F (23° C), 5 days

Secondary Fermentation: 59° F (15° C), 5 days

Also Noteworthy: Bottle conditioned

"Soon every bar wanted to get that cloudy beer you serve with a lemon, and the rest is history. The cloudy appearance and uniqueness of the combination made for an easy-drinking beer that was now special, a beer with character," Bryan said. "The domestic beer drinker was transitioning into craft with this brand, and given the relative lack of Midwestern competition from other craft breweries, we were able to dominate the category and grow very quickly into the brewery we are today."

Boulevard commissioned its new 150-barrel brew house in 2006, after squeezing 104,000 barrels out of its 35-barrel system in 2005. *Unfiltered Wheat* accounts for 65 percent of sales, wheat beers overall for 70 percent. Every weekday morning at 11 o'clock Pauwels and other brewers evaluate beers blind, and samples of *Unfiltered Wheat* are always in the mix. *UWB* is the top-selling craft beer in five Midwest states, and in Kansas City and several nearby metropolitan areas trails only *Bud Light* and *Miller Lite* in both number of tap handles and sales volume.

Comparing the basics for *UWB* and *ZÔN*, Boulevard's seasonal *wit* that won the gold medal at the 2009 Great American Beer Festival[SM], provides a lesson in cloudiness.

Unfiltered Wheat	**ZÔN**
(1.045) 11.3 °P	(1.043) 10.8 °P
4.4% abv	4.1% abv
56.5% pale malt	55% pale malt
19.5% raw wheat	22.5% raw wheat
22% malted wheat	22.5% malted wheat
2% percent Munich malt	

UWB mashing schedule:	**ZÔN mashing schedule:**
104° F (47° C) for 6.5 minutes	104° F (47° C) for 6.5 minutes
122° F (50° C) for 25 minutes	122° F (50° C) for 20 minutes
145° F (63° C) for 12 minutes	145° F (63° C) for 15 minutes
163° F (73° C) for 15 minutes	163° F (73° C) for 15 minutes
169° F (76° C) knockout	169° F (76° C) knockout

Of course, ZÔN also includes coriander and orange peel in the recipe, but the beers taste so different mostly because of the yeast. *Unfiltered Wheat* would taste of cloves and bananas were it fermented with a Bavarian *hefeweizen* yeast, and much like a Belgian-style *wit* were it fermented with a *wit* yeast. Boulevard uses an ale yeast originally sourced from England to ferment *Unfiltered Wheat* and most of its other beers.

The brewery hops *UWB* with a high-alpha variety (most recently, Simcoe) twice, once just before a 70-minute boil begins, the other 10 minutes in. "We just want 13 IBU," Pauwels said. Fermentation begins at 64° F (18° C), and when the gravity drops to 1.024 (6 °P) the temperature is raised to 73° F (23° C). Primary lasts 5 days, and after 5 days at 15° C, for stabilization, the beer is ready to bottle. It is centrifuged, then bottled with sugar and a dry yeast, less flocculent than the house yeast, and a modest 200,000 cells per milliliter. ("The yeast cells will grab the proteins and clear the beer," Pauwels said.) Conditioning usually takes 11 days, and the brewers carefully monitor to make sure no acetaldehyde (green apple) remains. By then about 2.5 volumes of CO_2 should have developed, with the idea it will reach 3 volumes in the marketplace.

Boulevard includes instructions on its cardboard carriers about how to pour a bottle of *Unfiltered Wheat*, calculating that because the process tosses particles back into solution, bottles have a shelf life of five months, compared to three months for kegs. Cloudiness begins to fade before flavor.

Pauwels grew up planning to be the local brewer in his hometown of Eeklo, north of Ghent and east of Brugge. However, brewing giant Interbrew closed the brewery the year after he completed his education in 1991, and as consolidation continued to eliminate breweries in Belgium, he started paying attention to what was happening in the United States. "I saw this movement and thought, 'I like this.' It was grassroots," he said. "There was nobody stopping these breweries from doing something new."

The only thing stopping Boulevard was capacity. The brewery didn't release a new full-time beer for nearly ten years because it couldn't keep up with demand, primarily for the *Unfiltered Wheat*. When the new brew house came online, that freed up the old one for a new Smokestack Series of beers, which includes four year-round selections and four seasonals, all specialty beers presented in 750-milliliter bottles.

Two Jokers Double Wit became the first wheat seasonal beer in the series. "The beer and the name is based on duality," Pauwels said. "On one side you have the old-school way of making a tart white beer, while on the other side you have the U.S. craft beer movement to make everything bigger, more complex. This beer is an approach to overcoming these differences."

Two Jokers begins with a sour mash. "I always thought that a sour mash was, with all respect, a homebrew way to make a sour beer without the bugs," Pauwels said. Then he read an article by Professor Hubert Verachtert of the University of Leuven, who wrote that white beer brewers at the turn of the century used a sour mash to minimize conversion and add acidity to the beer. "I like the idea of tartness in white beers. Nowadays we tend to over-spice these beers to reach that goal, while they were pretty simple beers at that time."

Pauwels said the key to the sour mash is to control the temperature and the amount of oxygen in the mash, making it as anaerobic as possible to minimize sharp acidic acid production. At Boulevard the brewers purge the mash tun with CO_2, mash-in at 95° F (35° C) and let the mash sit for 8 hours, so that the pH drops from 5.4 to 4.8.

"Then we raise the temperature as in a regular infusion mash. Take into account that amylase enzymes are less efficient at a lower pH and that you need to adjust your mash rest times," he said. "The nice thing about a sour mash is that you 'infect' your brew house and not the fermentation or aging area. The bacteria that are used to sour the mash come from the grain and are naturally in your mash already, and minimize the chance for cross contamination. You just give them the chance to get to work at the ideal temperature."

The sour mash produces most of the lactic character he wants, but he will add some to reach a target pH. He also adds citric acid, an ingredient likewise used in the late nineteenth century. "Lactic and citric acid create a different perception, and I like the sharper acidity," he said. *Two Jokers*, which is 8 percent alcohol by volume, is spiced with coriander, orange peel, lavender, cardamom, and grains of paradise, but none in quantities that make them easy to pick out.

"It's an American invention. Historically the only 'double *wit*' in Belgium was very light in alcohol," he said. "We thought, 'How can we do something that revives the old white tradition but is American?' "

License plates with beery messages decorate the Eccentric Café in Kalamazoo, where Bell's still maintains a small brewery.

A Midsummer's Night Dream

About five years after Kalamazoo Brewing, now Bell's Brewery, began making a wheat beer called *Solsun*, founder Larry Bell discovered the cloudy summer seasonal had taken on a life beyond the glass. The sororities at Western Michigan University, also in Kalamazoo, used the beer's logo on 600 T-shirts for fall rush.

"I realized I better get some trademark protection," Bell said. When he filed the papers, both Mexican brewing company Cerveceria Cuauhtemoc Moctezuma, which brewed a beer called *El Sol* (the Sun), and Canadian giant Molson opposed the application. Since Moctezuma had been around since 1890 Bell's lawyer suggested he could spend a million dollars fighting for the name and still lose. The good news was, Moctezuma would let Bell keep the distinctive logo.

He picked *Oberon* as the new name in 1996 because, in part, it also has six letters and the label was easy to change. "*Oberon* was sort of goofy, had some connotations," Bell said. "If you look at the Latin root, it means, 'they wander or go astray.' That seemed appropriate." Additionally, when Bell was a sixth-grader in Park Forest, Illinois, he played the part of Oberon, the fairy king, in Shakespeare's *A Midsummer Night's Dream*.

"I still have dinner with Queen Titania. She's looking pretty good," Bell said.

He bastardized the word "*saison*" when he first named *Solsun* in 1991 because the beer took its inspiration from the Belgian style. "We thought about what would we do in America and about using wheat," Bell said. Like many *saisons, Oberon* makes a spicy impression, although the recipe contains no spices. "We just used our house yeast, pretty simple. We sent it out for analysis, and it turns out it is pretty citrusy, so that works really well with this beer," Bell said.

Saaz hops, also part of the recipe since the first batch, add to the spicy character.

BELL'S OBERON
Original Gravity: 1.059 (14.5 °P)
Alcohol by Volume: 5.8%
Apparent Degree of Attenuation: 76%
IBU: 26
Malts: White wheat, pale, Munich
Hops: Saaz, Hersbrucker
Yeast: House
Fermentation schedule: Proprietary, out the door in 16 to 18 days

Oberon accounts for nearly half of Bell's production, about 130,000 barrels in 2009, although in the winter it is brewed only once a month for sale in southern states. Its return at the end of March each year has turned into an excuse for release parties in hundreds of spots across Michigan and elsewhere in the Midwest. During the following months the brewery may turn out eight batches of *Oberon,* along with several other brews, in a single day.

Bell began brewing multiple batches a day not long after he founded what was then called Kalamazoo Brewing in 1984, today the oldest microbrewery east of Colorado. Of course, those were one-barrel batches, a step up from the 15-gallon soup kettle he started brewing in. Then, he was the lone full-time employee. Now, the quality control lab has two full-time employees.

Bell renamed the brewery after he built a new facility just outside of town in 2003. Then, the brew house produced a new batch every four hours. Now, it can drop a new mash every ninety minutes, and there are twenty-four-hour stretches where sixteen batches head for fermenters. "Every year we try to take out a weak link," brew house manager Ken Belau said in July 2008.

Shift manager Andy Farrell was sitting at a computer screen, monitoring the progress of several batches at once. Farrell pulled up the recipes for *Oberon*—two, because one of the reasons the system is so efficient is it has two lauter tuns, and the recipe is a little different for each. He illustrated what he does when the system spots a problem. He popped open a screen that showed a list of recent alarms. Some were false; for some the solution was obvious, but for others a decision had to be made. Farrell took action at the keyboard, but if he had to he could walk over to the brew house and fix almost any problem with his hands. Instead, he touched the necessary valves using a mouse.

"Systems are most efficient when they are running at a steady state," production manager John Mallett said, explaining why and how Bell's continues to produce a rather insane amount of beer with a 50-barrel brew house. "We want to be able to support all these little brands we make and deliver them super fresh." *Oberon* is no small brand, of course, but freshness matters more than it does for one of Bell's famous stouts.

Although Mallett takes obvious pride in the fact that almost every bit of equipment in Bell's growing brewery did service somewhere else first, the laboratory is fully stocked. "Microbiology is super important when you don't filter," Nicholas said. Mallett, who has 5-liter kegs of *Oberon* sitting above his desk, talked about the role consumers play. "You begin by putting the haze up front, and you talk to them about rousing it," he said.

"We spend a lot of our time focusing on fermentation, so that we're always delivering the same beer to the bottling line, that it's homogeneous and with a set yeast load," he said. "As we've gotten bigger we've gotten more consistent with process and more insight into our process."

The boss is impressed. Larry Bell didn't need a second to consider the question about whether *Oberon* tastes the same today as *Solsun* did in the early 1990s.

"No," he said, laughing loud and long. "We got rid of all the diacetyl and butterscotch we had in it."

Summer Ale on the Oregon Coast

Distraction comes easily at Pelican Pub & Brewery in Pacific City, Oregon, hard on the Pacific Ocean and with a closeup view of one of the several haystack rocks along Oregon's coast. Spend a few moments gazing at nearby Cape Kiwanda and look back down at samples of the brewpub's beers, and you might not be sure which is *Surfer's Summer Ale* and which is *Kiwanda Cream Ale.*

Both are golden, and it happens they have almost the same original gravity, alcohol by volume, and bitterness units. Yet the only things they share are the yeast and the water they are brewed with. *Kiwanda Cream* is a classic, clean and a bit green, sweet and not quite bitter. *Summer Ale* has more texture, a combination of crackers and chewy bread, a lesson in what wheat adds to a beer not labeled a "wheat beer."

Pelican brewmaster Darron Welch first made *Surfer's Summer Ale* because he had an 11-pound box of hops in need of a beer. He picked up free English First Gold hops at a trade show in 2002. "I thought, 'Now what do I do?' I didn't want to mess up *Kiwanda* or another of our brands," he said.

He had read that something called summer ale was an "emerging style" in England, so he began digging deeper. "From looking at the specs you can infer an awful lot. That allowed me to make an assumption about bitterness and mouthfeel," Welch said. The following year, after he had brewed his own interpretation, Welch tasted *Hopback Summer Lightning* for the first time at the 2003 Real Ale Festival in Chicago. That beer had been runner-up for Champion Beer of Britain at the 2001 Great British Beer Festival.

"I thought, 'Holy smoke, my idea of what the style should be actually resembles *Summer Lightning*,'" Welch said. He later mentioned the experience to Charlie Papazian, who, as president of the Brewers Association continues to be active in writing guidelines for the Great American Beer Festival and World Beer Cup competitions. Welch's research became the basis for the Summer Ale style.

Welch includes 70 percent Simpson's Golden Promise in *Surfer's Summer Ale,* 25 percent malted white wheat and 5 percent torrified red wheat. Golden Promise provides the biscuit and "almost silky" character, while wheat adds bready character. He began using Glacier hops, grown nearby, in his third batch. American ale yeast ferments this beer as well as several others. "It takes about five generations to adapt, then we got thirty on top of that," he said.

He dry hops *Summer Ale* for about three days, during the diacetyl rest, and it's ready to serve after a few more days in a unitank. Welch views wheat as just another ingredient in this particular beer, unlike another summer seasonal, *Organic Heiferweizen*, a *wit* brewed with malted wheat, flaked (red) wheat, and flaked barley. "I like the red wheat for this beer, more protein, more of the right protein," he said. "It makes our beer cloudy."

You wouldn't mistake *Heiferweizen* for *Surfer's Summer Ale*, but sometimes customers complain it isn't cloudy enough. "We're in the land of *Widmer Hefeweizen*," Welch said.

SURFER'S SUMMER ALE
Original Gravity: 1.049 (12.2 °P)
Alcohol by Volume: 5.3%
Apparent Degree of Attenuation: 83%
IBU: 25
Malts: Golden Promise, white wheat, torrified wheat
Hops: Glacier
Yeast: House pale ale
Primary Fermentation: 66° F (19° C), 5 days
Secondary Fermentation: 3 to 4 days, then crashed
Also Noteworthy: Lightly dry hopped

Wheat Wine: The Beer

Everybody agrees that Phil Moeller at Rubicon Brewing in Sacramento, California, brewed the first wheat wine in 1988, taking inspiration from a homebrewed wheat ale that accidentally turned out too strong (isn't that the way it always works?). Seventeen years later the idea a beer might be called "wheat wine" was still news to the federal government. When Smuttynose Brewing in New Hampshire took steps to bottle its *Wheat Wine Ale* in 2005, the Tax and Trade Bureau rejected the label application on the grounds that the use of the word "wine" in a beer name would confuse consumers. Smuttynose persevered, and other breweries since have followed with bottled versions of their own, together illustrating a broad range of approaches to brewing a wheat wine.

For instance, vintages of Smuttynose have ranged from 10.3 percent alcohol by volume to 11.4 percent, contain about 70 IBU, and are dry hopped and aged on oak chips. *Star Brew* from Marin Brewing in California is 9.2 percent and packed with intense American hop character (citrus and pine). New Holland Brewing in Michigan describes its wheat wine, *Pilgrim's Dole,* as a "barleywine-style ale made with 50 percent wheat." Brewmaster John Haggerty said the wort is boiled for two and a half hours to promote caramelization, with a typical batch fermented with the house ale yeast starting at 1.101 to 1.105 (24 to 25 °P) and finishing 1.017 to 1.018 (4.3 to 4.5 °P). *Pilgrim's Dole* then ages at least 180 days in Bourbon barrels, typically "third-use" following two batches of the strong ale called *Dragon's Milk.* The 2009 vintage measured 11.36 percent alcohol by volume with 70 IBU.

RUBICON WINTER WHEAT WINE
Original Gravity: 1.126 (29.4 °P)
Alcohol by Volume: 12%
Apparent Degree of Attenuation: 72%
IBU: 60
Malts: Wheat, Golden Promise, crystal
Hops: German Magnum, Spalt, Saaz or Tettnang
Yeast: House ale yeast
Primary Fermentation: Held at 68° F (20° C), about 7 days
Secondary Fermentation: 32° F (0° C), 3 weeks
Also Noteworthy: 6 to 8 weeks old before it is served

Rubicon makes *Winter Wheat Wine* once a year, generally aiming for between 10.5 to 11 percent alcohol by volume. Brewmaster Scott Cramlet had his 2008 batch analyzed by White Labs, and it came in at 12 percent alcohol by volume and 60 IBU. He packs his 10-barrel mash tun twice and boils twice to make a single batch. In 2008 one half started at 1.137 (31.8 °P) and the other at 1.115 (27 °P)—combining for 1.126 (29.4 °P), when 1.115 to 1.119 (27 to 28 °P) would be more common. The grist contained 57 percent wheat, Simpson's Golden Promise, and a small measure of crystal malt. Cramlet does a single-infusion mash at a relatively low 147 to 148° F (64 to 65° C), figuring, "there's so much extract the beer will have plenty of body."

For that 2008 batch the boil reduced one half from 280 gallons down to 160 gallons over the course of nearly 5 hours, then the other from 260 to 170 in a little less time. He uses all noble hops, "just like Phil Moeller did," currently bittering it with German Magnum, adding Spalt at the end of the boil, and dry hopping it with Czech Saaz or German Tettnang.

He pitches double his normal amount of American ale yeast at 68° F (20° C) and holds the temperature for about a week. When fermentation is finished, he chills the fermenter to 32° F (0° C), and *Winter Wheat* sits for 3 weeks. Then he moves the beer into a bright tank and fines it, waiting "until it feels right" to serve it, usually about 6 to 8 weeks. In the 1990s the brewpub sold *Winter Wheat Wine* by the pitcher but doesn't any more. Cramlet runs the beer into kegs when the serving tank begins to empty, saving some for special events like the Great American Beer Festival. It won gold at the 2006 GABF and in the 2008 World Beer Cup.

A Beer for the Punk Comic Crowd

Jonathan Cutler at Piece Brewery & Pizzeria might be more candid than most brewers when he talks about the wheat ale he makes for summer consumption at the Chicago brewpub. "I call it our bullshit American wheat ale," he said. Cutler brews award-winning *hefeweizens* (pages 102-103), but he puts his beer brewed with 25 percent wheat, American hops, and an English ale yeast on tap in the summer for those who want something even lighter in color and flavor than the *weizen*.

Making a wheat beer the house light beer has been standard practice at brewpubs for twenty years, which is why Nick Floyd of Three Floyds Brewing in Indiana is just getting warmed up when he says, "Most American wheat beer is boring. For me (American wheat) is the *Miller Lite* of the brewpub chains." He brewed *Gumballhead* to prove "American wheat beer doesn't suck."

Gumballhead is made with pale malt, red wheat, and aromatic malt, hopped with Warrior, Simcoe, and Amarillo and fermented with Three Floyds' house pale ale yeast. It's the same yeast Cutler uses in the summer wheat ale at Piece (he and Floyd are friends), as a matter of fact. In *Gumballhead* serious hop flavor plays off light, spicy wheat character on the palate. Floyd is known for favoring hops—each year during the Great American Beer Festival, breweries across the nation compete to see who brews the best hop-centric beer in a contest named after Three Floyds flagship *Alpha King*—and in this beer reserves most of the charge for flavor and aroma, adding more hops at the end of the boil and dry hopping after fermentation is complete.

THREE FLOYDS GUMBALLHEAD
Original Gravity: 1.053 (13.5 °P)
Alcohol by Volume: 5.5%
Apparent Degree of Attenuation: 76%
IBU: 28
Malts: Pale two-row, red wheat, aromatic
Hops: Amarillo, Warrior, Simcoe
Yeast: House pale ale yeast
Primary Fermentation: 70° F (21° C), 3 to 4 days
Secondary Fermentation: 3 weeks at 32° F (0° C)

Gumballhead pours just a bit hazy. "Our yeast flocs (flocculates) so well, people can't believe it's not filtered," Floyd said. "I don't want it to look like a *wit* beer." He first brewed it as a summer seasonal in 2004, available only on draft. "We had *Extra Pale Ale.* Good, but kind of boring. I wanted a good standout summer beer people would remember," he said. The following summer Three Floyds also sold the beer in 22-ounce bottles. "People were clamoring for six-packs," Floyd said. At the same time he made the beer available year-round, and now, in some months, *Gumballhead* sells almost as well as *Alpha King.*

The distinctive *Gumballhead* logo was drawn by Rob Syers, who founded the Skin Graft punk-comic zine, which morphed into an independent record company that sometimes wraps its releases in comics featuring Gumballhead the Cat.

Not a label you'd wrap around a boring beer.

chapter eleven
TWO RECIPES FOR WHEAT WINE

"There is no grape wine, but wine is made of wheat and rice with many spices, and a very good drink it is."

– Travels With Marco Polo

Why would anybody want to make wine out of wheat? Because, according to United States Patent 4675192, wineries that use fresh grapes can produce only a few months during the year, but wineries that use wheat can produce all year. The patent, filed in 1987, described a resulting product that would be "a slightly sweet white wine having a taste which was reported to make one think of a cluster of ripe dew-covered grapes."

In 1988 Phil Moeller at Rubicon Brewing came up with a better idea, a "wheat wine" made with beer ingredients. Apparently nobody has tried to patent that, which is probably just as well given that it is a "style" in progress. According to Sacramento legend, a local home-brewer's mistake—he was aiming for a "summer wheat ale" but ended up with a beer stronger than 10 percent alcohol by volume—inspired Moeller to make the first wheat wine. It since has won gold at both the Great American Beer Festival and World Beer Cup, judged against these guidelines:

"American style wheat wines range from gold to deep amber and are brewed with 50 percent or more wheat malt. They have full body and

Steven Pauwels. Photo courtesy of Boulevard Brewing.

Todd Ashman. Photo courtesy of Todd Ashman.

high residual malty sweetness. Bitterness is moderate to low. Fruity-ester characters are often high and counterbalanced by complexity of alcohols and high alcohol content. Hop aroma and flavor are at low to medium levels."

That's one choice. Here we have two more. When Steven Pauwels, brewmaster at Boulevard Brewing, began working on a recipe for a new beer he eventually would call *Harvest Dance Wheat Wine*, he looked at that description and shook his head. "I cannot make a beer like that," he said.

"Why would I make this beer? I want wine flavors in there, not to make a barley wine with a wheat portion," he said. He thought about how Citra, a relatively new hop with Sauvignon Blanc characteristics, would add "grapy, tropical fruit flavors and aromas" to complement a bit of fruitiness from Belgian yeast used in several of the Smokestack beers. Next he went looking for more wine flavors, from oak and from grapes. He aged part of the wheat wine in barrels that once held Viognier wine, then he used grape juice as his fuel for refermentation in the bottle.

In contrast, Todd Ashman of FiftyFifty Brewing in Truckee, California, likes a wheat wine with bold American hops, much like *420 Wheat*

Wine, which won accolades when he was brewing at Flossmoor Station in Illinois. "I still lump it in with the barley wine category. You want those American hops, but the wheat character should be apparent," he said.

He's partial to red wheat because of the bit of tartness it should add, and a small portion of unmalted flaked wheat is intended to give it an attractive head and rich mouthfeel. "I want that good mouthfeel but I don't want it to be caramel," he said, describing how he thinks wheat wine should differ from barley wine. "You'll get some of that from the boil, but this should have a pleasant graininess, a cleaner flavor than you get with just malt."

Steve Pauwels' Wheat Wine Recipe
Original Gravity: 1.083 to 1.087 (20 to 21 °P)
Final Gravity: 1.016 to 1.017 (4 to 4.4 °P)
Alcohol by Volume: 8.5-9.5%
IBU: 38
Grain Bill:
Pale malt or blend of domestic pale malt and Pilsener malt 47% (we use 37% pale malt and 10% Pilsener malt)
Malted wheat (white wheat) 25%
Raw wheat (soft red wheat) 22%
Carawheat 2%
Golden Naked Oats 2%
Amber malt 2%

Mashing:
Add an organic acid to your mash to get pH between 5.2 and 5.4. With a high percentage of wheat a protein rest is favorable.
Mash-in 126 to 129° F (52 to 54° C), rest for 20 minutes
Raise temperature to 145° F (63° C) for 60 minutes
Mash-off at 163 to 167° F (73 to 75° C)
Use rice hulls if necessary to improve lautering

Hops:
Hallertau Magnum or Tradition, first wort (7 IBU)
Hallertau Magnum or Tradition, 90 minutes (9 IBU)
Citra or Nelson Sauvin, 10 minutes (16 IBU)

Citra or Nelson Sauvin, heat off or whirlpool (6 IBU)
Boil: 90 minutes. Add dextrose to the boil to get to 1.083 (20 °P) minimum.
Yeast: A Belgian yeast strain that is low in 4-vinyl guaiacol formation, alcohol tolerant, and low to medium ester producer
Fermentation: Ferment at low range until 1.028 (7 °P) left. Then let fermentation temperature increase to make sure fermentation finishes completely and diacetyl is below threshold. Cool down to 32 to 36° F (0 to 2° C) and let age on oak (chips or spirals). Use medium toast to get oak aroma and vanilla notes. Use heavier toasted oak if you prefer honey, coffee, and caramelized flavors.
Bottling: Bottle condition with grape juice to increase complexity of the beer. Concentrated grape juice has 68° Brix or 68 grams sugar per 100-gram solution. Fresh juice from a vineyard will be between 22 and 24° Brix.

Todd Ashman's Wheat Wine Recipe
Original Gravity: 1.103 to 1.110 (24.5 to 26 °P)
Final Gravity: 1.018 to 1.024 (4.5 to 6 °P)
Alcohol by Volume: 9-10.5%
IBU: 65-80

Grain Bill:
Domestic and/or imported two-row base malt 63%
Red wheat malt 27%
Belgian aromatic malt or Gambrinus honey malt 5%
CaraPils or similar low-color crystal malt 2.5%
Unmalted red wheat or flaked wheat 2.5%

Mashing:
Treat water same as you would for a barley wine or an IPA. Mash temperature should be in the 156-157° F (70° C) range for adequate body for this big beer. Get a fair amount of the base malt mashed in prior to sending in the wheat; this will allow a nice bed of husks to build up, and there should not be a problem with runoff. Sparge at 167° F (75° C) and run off at a moderate rate.

Hops:

Centennial, 90 minutes (60 IBU)

Amarillo, 30 minutes (10 IBU)

Cascade, 10 minutes (5 IBU)

Cascade, heat off or whirlpool (quantity equal to the 10-minute addition)

Boil: 90 minutes

Yeast: Your preferred yeast strain for barley wine. Something neutral and alcohol tolerant.

Fermentation: Ferment at 68 to 70° F (20 to 21° C) or recommended temperature of yeast provider. Let beer finish completely, and diacetyl rest as well. Cool to 32° F (0° C), and age for at least 3 weeks and preferably longer, allowing flavors to develop completely.

PART V:
WHEAT BEERS FROM THE PAST

chapter twelve
BEERS THE REINHEITSGEBOT NEVER MET

"Whereas weissbier makes the drinker monosyllabic, reserved, and retiring, the Bavarian brewings open his heart and let loose his tongue."
— Henry Vizetelly

The last brewery in Berlin producing Berliner *weisse*, and therefore the last brewery on Earth that may use the appellation, does not feature the historic beer during tours. However, when visitors reach a small, well-appointed pub deep within the brewery, they will see several old but full bottles of Berliner *weisse* from a variety of former producers sitting behind the small bar.

The tour includes a meal accompanied by a choice of beers, all made by breweries within the massive Radeberger group that owns the consolidated Berliner-Kindl-Schultheiss brewery. Within a few hours on this December afternoon two groups, totaling about two dozen people, will pass through, but I won't see anybody order a Berliner *weisse*. Two men talk about *Schöfferhofer Hefeweizen Mix-Grapefruit*. "I only smelled it. I didn't inhale," one tells the other.

When the tour guide pulls down several bottles so I can take a closer look at these antiques, that man, from Berlin, volunteers that his brother-in-law recently opened an eighteen-year-old bottle of *Schultheiss Berliner Weisse* and offered him some. "He said it tasted like Champagne, but I don't drink *weissbier*," he says. "It did *look* like Champagne."

Two hundred years after Napoleon's soldiers described Berliner *weisse* as sweet and tart, strong and effervescent, "the Champagne of the North," we won't be opening one of these dusty bottles. Instead I try a new offering from the brewery, *Berliner Kindl Weisse* mixed with black currant juice in the bottle. Perhaps it would have been better had it aged a few years.

A proper history of northern German brewing includes many unusual beers, some made with wheat, most of which have fallen by the wayside. That some would have violated the Reinheitsgebot doesn't matter, because the rest of Germany did not adopt the Bavarian "beer purity" law until 1906, and even then with loopholes. The two most prominent survivors, Berliner *weisse* and Leipziger Gose, don't enjoy the popularity they once did in their home cities, but those are still the best places to learn about them.

Although a decree establishing a special tax on Berlin's *weissbier* in 1680 serves as something of a birth certificate, nothing indicates that, at the time, the city's beer would have been any different from those from Hamburg or Nürnberg. Accounts simply describe "mildly tasty beers," with no mention of the lactic flavors that would later make them famous. In describing the brewing process in 1765 Johann Samuel Halle wrote that at least some brewers sought to find a way to produce a *Weisbierhefe* that would not turn sour. Even so, he suggested that the beer should be served within eight days after leaving the brewery in summer and fourteen in winter.[1]

Both J.G. Krünitz (in *Oekonomische Encyklopädie*) and Halle described the brewing process used in the second half of the eighteenth century, both indicating production was brewery-specific. For instance, Halle offered a recipe made with equal parts of barley and wheat malts, while Krünitz provided one with two-thirds wheat. Such differences continued until only two breweries made the beer at the beginning of

[1] Gerolf Annemüller, Hans-J. Manger, and Peter Lietz, *Die Berliner Weisse: Ein Stück Berliner Geschichte* (Berlin: VLBFachbücher, 2001), 34.

the twenty-first century, because until they merged, Berliner Kindl and Schultheiss followed very different processes.

From the beginning Berlin's brewers sought to keep the beers as white as possible. Air-dried or lightly kilned wheat worked particularly well, although it's not clear if the brewers of the time understood the microbiological implications—further exacerbated by minimizing the impact of hops. Krünitz wrote about a process in which brewers pulled off the thinnest portion of a mash from the top and brought it to a boil, then added hops. The remaining wort was never boiled. (To this day the brewers of *Berliner Kindl Weisse* split the wort, don't boil half at all, and add hops only to the other half).

Oekonomische Encyklopädie described a yeast strain that generated a curious by-product: "After five or six hours, when the fermentation goes well, a white spot appears in the middle of the beer, and the *weissbier* brewer then usually puts his beer immediately into barrels, without waiting for a full fermentation in the mash tun. The beer is taken into the cellar and here it must ferment or, as they say, belch. First sticky and pitchlike yeast appears, which consequently in Berlin is called pitch or pitch barm. Cobblers use this yeast as glue. The *weissbier* brewer has to carefully remove this yeast and isolate it from the yeast used for pitching." The brewer would use this yeast in a new batch but alternate reusing his own yeast with yeast acquired elsewhere. *Weissbier* was seldom sold on draft but delivered to publicans, who filled bottles themselves. [2]

In *Die Herstellung Obergähriger Biere,* Dr. Franz Schönfeld also reported the practice of periodically acquiring new yeast continued well into the nineteenth century. *Weissbier* brewers regularly refreshed their yeast because "if they kept repitching harvested yeast, their beer was too sour. "[3] Schönfeld also wrote:

- Before 1850 most Berliner *weisse* was sold a day or two after being brewed. The beer was finished by publicans, who also bottled it. This practice continued into the twentieth century.
- Brewers began using mixed cultures in the 1830s or 1840s that could safely be repitched without being periodically refreshed.

[2] Ronald Pattinson, *Decoction!* (Amsterdam: Kilderkin, 2008), 82-83.

[3] Pattinson, Decoction!, 87.

- Berliner *weisse* was often watered down at bottling time, which became illegal in the twentieth century.
- Until the 1860s smoked wheat malt was used to brew Berliner *weisse*. Then one brewer experimented with an unsmoked version that was so well received by drinkers that other brewers quickly followed suit.
- Between 1892 and 1897 the number of top-fermenting breweries in Berlin increased from forty-seven to seventy-one.

That revival followed a twenty-year period beginning in the late 1850s when Berliner *weisse* fell so out of favor that one Englishman predicted, "Ten years hence and guide-books will describe [*weissbier*] with the same reverence as the Colosseum in Rome, or the Palace of the Doges in Venice. Ten years later there will be a case in the Berlin Museum containing the mysterious goblets, representing a 'white or a half white,' and the so-called 'cool blonde.' "[4]

Henry Vizetelly, an English publisher who also wrote about wine, paid homage to the "Kühle Blonde" in *Berlin Under the New Empire,* describing in detail its place in a Berliner's life. "Characteristic among Berlin drinking establishments are the *Wein-stube* and the *Weissbier* Saloon, both usually to be met within the quieter streets and frequented by regular rather than by chance customers," he wrote. He described publicans uncorking stone bottles and pouring beer into huge glasses. "In front of everyone stood a gigantic tumbler which could have been fitted with ease upon any ordinary head, and which contained a liquid pale and clear as Rhine wine, surmounted by a huge crown of froth not unlike a prize cauliflower," he continued. "This was the famous 'weiss,' the mere mention of which suffices to send a Berliner into raptures and into the mysteries of which I was about to be initiated." Berlin was "the city where the *kühle blonde* is obtained in the greatest perfection and where *bier-stuben* offering no other beverage to their frequenters abound. The beer is drunk by preference when it is of a certain age, and in perfection it should be largely impregnated with carbonic acid gas and have acquired a peculiar sharp, dry, and by no means disagreeable flavor."[5]

[4] Richard Bentley, et al., *Bentley's Miscellany*, Vol. 46 (London: Richard Bentley, 1859), 418.

[5] Henry Vizetelly, *Berlin Under the New Empire* (London: Tinsley Brothers, 1879), 310-311.

Vizetelly described regular *weissbier* drinkers starting with a nip of *kummel* (caraway liqueur), but otherwise did not mention colored syrups. Unlike eschewing a lemon garnish with *weizen* to avoid looking like a beer tourist in the south, embracing a red or green *Kindl Weiss* will make you appear to be a local in Berlin. As Michael Jackson explained in *The World Guide to Beer* in 1977, " 'White' is a particular misnomer for a beer which is usually drunk either red or green. However delightful they may find the beer itself, visitors from other countries are apt to be shocked by these colors, but Germans are frequently surprised at the thought of drinking a Berliner *weisse* without a *schuss* (a dash of raspberry juice) or *Waldmeister* (essence of woodruff)." Radeberger even sells the blends premixed, and advertisements picture a bent straw protruding from large bowl-shaped glasses associated with the beer.

Vizetelly wrote that "Bavarian" beers held the place of honor in Berlin in the 1870s, with thirty-four breweries producing beers using "fermentation from below," such as bock ("two gallons, it is said, are needed to make a Bavarian unsteady, whilst two mugsful suffice to intoxicate a stranger"). In 1879 sixteen breweries made Berliner *weisse,* with ten brewing "Bitterbier" and five "Braunbier," thick and sweet, considered more nourishing than intoxicating. Two breweries made something called Berliner *Weizenbier,* a wheat beer brewed without hops. He estimated Berlin breweries produced between 40 million and 50 million gallons, or 50 gallons per resident, compared to 10 gallons per head for the rest of Prussia. [6]

Through most of its history Berliner *weisse* qualified as a *shankbier*, low in alcohol and taxed at a lower rate. German law requires the starting gravity of *shankbier* must be between 1.028 and 1.032 (7 °P to 8 °P), producing a beer of about 3 percent alcohol by volume. However, stronger versions once existed, as confirmed by M. Krandauer in 1914 (along with the fact that beers continued to be brewed stronger and watered down at bottling).

"After the end of the tun fermentation the beer is pumped into a collecting vat, from which together with fresh beer from the pitching vessel it is drawn off into smaller packages, bottles, or stone jugs," he wrote. "It is worth mentioning that this mixture of finished and fresh beer contains

---

[6] Vizetelly, *Berlin*, 331-332.

between 10 and 35 percent water, depending on the wishes of the consumer. Hence the designation 'half beer' as opposed to 'full *weisse*' or 'whole *weisse*,' beer without added water. An exception, approximately like Bock or Salvator in bottom-fermenting beers, amongst *Weissbiers* is formed by '*Märzen-Bier*,' which because of its winelike flavor is very highly regarded."

He reported starting gravities of 1.048 (12 °P), 1.058 (14 °P), and 1.068 (16 °P). "This beer conditions in the bottle without the addition of water. It takes months before the beer is ready to be consumed," he wrote. "Often the custom still prevails of burying the bottles in sand or earth to keep them at a constant cool temperature." [7]

As late as the 1950s, Rudolf Dicksheit documented that brewers in the German Democratic Republic (East Germany) sometimes made 1.048 (12 °P) Berliner *weissbiers* along with a more typical *shankbier*. Dicksheit described a process nominally changed during the first half of the twentieth century. The grist contained widely ranging percentages of wheat, from 50 percent to 80 percent. Many began to boil the wort to avoid infection, but only briefly. An infusion mash was common—since the eighteenth century some brewers had used infusion, others still conducted as many as three decoctions—beginning at 122° F (50° C) with saccharification at 156° F (69° C). Brewers boiled the wort for 15 to 30 minutes, then transferred it to a coolship for 20 minutes. It was cooled to 68 to 71° F (20 to 22° C) and pitched with yeast.

Primary fermentation lasted 30 to 48 hours at 64° to 68° F (18° to 20° C). The young beer was mixed immediately with about 15 percent kraeusen and transferred to bottles or barrels, with some pubs still bottling beer after receiving kegs. Bottles lagering at the brewery rested at 59° F (15° C). If the cellar temperature dropped lower than that, secondary conditioning progressed too slowly, as did clarification.

"*Weissbier* yeast is a mixture, living in symbiosis, of top-fermenting beer yeast and lactic acid bacteria, which multiply greatly during the fermentation process, so that the proportion is about 1:1," Dicksheit wrote. "The bacteria die during storage also relatively more quickly. The ratio of yeast to lactic acid bacteria changes then to around 4:1. . . . The lactic acid bacteria in Berliner *weissbier* yeast is not a single strain, but many strains which coexist." [8]

[7] Pattinson, *Decoction!*, 73.

[8] Pattinson, *Decoction!*, 103.

Dicksheit provided details about a failed attempt to produce a Berliner *weissbier* yeast in which top-fermenting beer yeast and *Lactobacillus delbrückii* bacteria were brought together. "This yeast-lactic acid bacteria mixture did not produce the characteristic Berliner *Weissbier* aroma," he wrote. "It is also very difficult to accustom the two types of organism to a symbiosis."

Max Delbrück, a Berlin native who moved to the United States in 1937 and later became more famous for his Nobel Prize-winning work in medicine, had isolated the *Lactobacillus delbrückii* strain in the 1930s. This provided brewers with greater understanding of the relationship between *Saccharomyces cerevisiae* and lactic acid bacteria during fermentation.

Not until the second half of the twentieth century did brewing scientists identify *Brettanomyces* in Berliner *weisse*. F.J. Methner showed that the mixed pitching cultures contained *Brett* and a second variety could be found, passed on through brewery equipment. The slow-acting strains affected flavor and aroma only in bottles cellared for an extended period.

BERLINER KINDL WEISSE
Original Gravity: 1.029 (7.5 °P)
Alcohol by Volume: 2.9%
Apparent Degree of Attenuation: 78%
IBU: 4
Malts: 3 parts Pilsener, 1 part wheat
Hops: Northern Brewer
Yeast: *Saccharomyces* for one half, *Lactobacillus* (80 liters for 800 hectoliters) for the other
Primary Fermentation: Yeasts pitched at 59° F (15° C), rises to 77° F (21° C), 1 week
Secondary Fermentation: Halves combined and conditioned cold
Also Noteworthy: Flash pasteurized, no longer bottle conditioned

Berliner Kindl Weisse is a relatively small brand in the massive Radeberger portfolio, accounting for about 60,000 hectoliters (51,000 barrels) of the 1.6 million hectoliters made at the gleaming Berliner-Kindl-Schultheiss brewery. The brewery sells the *Berliner Pilsner, Berliner Kindl,* and Schultheiss brands only in the immediate region, except for *Berliner Kindl Weisse,* which is available nationally but no longer exported. Production of *Schultheiss Weisse* ended in 2006.

Although Radeberger responds to inquiries about production of *Kindl Weisse* with a statement that "the technology details, the ingredients, and the exact recipe are secrets strictly kept by our brewmasters," during a tour that focuses on the production of *Pilsner* those at work in the brewery are less secretive. They reveal the *Weisse* contains one part wheat malt to three parts barley. The brewers take half the wort, don't boil it, don't add hops and infuse it with *Lactobacillus delbrückii* (80 liters in an 800-hectoliter, or 520-barrel, tank, to give you an idea of the scale of production). They boil the other half with the tiniest portion of hops and ferment it with *Saccharomyces.* Then the two are blended. The brewery began flash pasteurizing *Kindl Weisse* in 2006, discontinuing traditional bottle conditioning and reducing the CO_2 in bottles from 4 volumes to 2.75.

The best place to drink Gose must be Ohne Bedenken, the Leipzig *Gosenschenke* (Gose house) so essential in resurrecting this defunct style of sour wheat beer spiced with coriander and salt. It's a multi-room tavern with long tables and cozy nooks, a virtual shrine to a time in the nineteenth century when university students would have greased their conversations with a glass of Gose. To understand how it's made in a modern brewery, head to Bayerischer Bahnhof Gasthaus and Gose Brauerei, less than three miles away.

Some tables at the brewpub offer a view inside Bahnhof brewmaster Matthias Richter's kettles, and while he's at work he can see what customers are drinking. "We have people from Leipzig who are drinking only Gose in this pub," he said, pronouncing the name of the beer "goes-a" with a short "a" at the end. "People from other towns will come to try it. But in Germany most people drink *pils.* They will try Gose, then change back to *pils.*"

Richter heard about Gose in brewing school but had never tasted the style before he went to work at Bayerischer Bahnhof in 2003. Little wonder—the last Gose brewery (before a revival) closed in 1966, although a series of breweries produced small batches under contract beginning in 1985. Not until Bayerischer Bahnhof opened in 1999 was one committed to ongoing production.

Brewing in the town of Goslar, about 150 miles south of Hamburg and 115 northeast of Leipzig, seems to date to the first millennia. Three hundred breweries, probably most of them in homes, operated by 1500, and during the seventeenth century German writers identified Goslar as an important brewing center because of its specialty beer called *gosa*.[9] They listed it beside beers such as Braunschweig *mumme* and Hanover *Broyhan*, which we know were sometimes tart.

Michael Jackson wrote about a potential connection between the Belgian *gueuze* and Gose (which, he noted, would be pronounced much the same if Gose had an umlaut over the "o"), and research by Yvan De Baets (page 42) further suggests the possibility. What Gose tasted like before the eighteenth century remains lost in the cloud of history, but by 1740 one description alludes to spontaneous fermentation, stating "Gose ferments itself without the addition of yeast." It was also said to have laxative qualities that inspired this rhyme:

> *"Es ist war ein gutes Biere die Goslarische Gose,*
> *doch wenn man meint, sie sei im Bauch,*
> *so liegt sie in der Hose."*

Translation: "It is indeed a good beer, Goslar Gose; though when you think it is in your belly, so it is in your trousers."

Leipzig taverns began selling Gose "imported" from Goslar in about 1740, and soon various *Gosenschenke* demanded still more of the beer. Leipzig-area breweries, notably in the small town of Döllnitz, began making it as well. Breweries held their recipes and production records close, so we don't have the sort of production detail to point to as with Berliner *weisse*. The use of lactic acid bacteria indicates, however, that not all fermentation was spontaneous.

History also confirms the unusual importance publicans played in the final product. Breweries delivered still-fermenting Gose to pubs in barrels. Tavern owners knew the beer was ready to bottle when yeast quit spilling

---

[9] Richard W. Unger, *Beer in the Middle Ages and the Renaissance* (Philadelphia: University of Pennsylvania Press, 2004), 192.

out a shive hole on the keg. They filled the longneck flasks unique to Gose, allowing the foam that rose into the neck to act as a stopper. Bahnhof packages a portion of its Gose in similar bottles, but closes them with a flip-top stopper. The *Gosenschenke* owner would further condition the beer at least a week, but with an eye toward the thermometer, because a beer could turn bad within three weeks in summer.

Gose sold at a premium to other beers, so even though as many as eighty Gose houses operated around 1900 it remained a specialty, one that suffered the same fate as many other styles that were not golden lager in the twentieth century. Following World War II, when brewing halted, only one small brewery in Leipzig, Friedrich Wurzler Brauerei, made Gose. Wurzler had worked before the war at the legendary Rittergutsbrauerei brewery in Döllnitz, which in 1945 was confiscated and closed. Ron Pattinson offers a bittersweet story about what followed:

"After landing in Leipzig during the war, he was able to start his own brewery, mostly based on the handwritten notebook in his possession, which explained the secret of brewing Gose. Before his death in the late 1950s, he handed on the secret to his stepson, Guido Pfnister. Brewing of Gose continued in the small private brewery, though there appears to have been little demand. By the 1960s there were no more than a couple of pubs in Leipzig and possibly one in Halle that were still selling it.

"Gose struggled along until 1966, when, while working in his garden, Guido Pfnister had a heart attack and died. The local nationalised group, VEB Sachsenbräu, had no interest in taking over the small, run-down Wurzler brewery, and so it was closed. Another small private brewery, Brauerei Ermisch, considered continuing the production of Gose and took possession of Pfnister's brewing book. Their enthusiasm didn't last long, and not only was no Gose produced, but the notebook also appeared to have been accidentally destroyed." [10]

That didn't turn out to be the end of the story. To properly restore Leipzig's most famous *Gosenschenke*, Ohne Bedenken, in the mid-1980s owner Lothar Goldhahn decided he needed to be able to sell a genuine Gose. He located a former employee of the Wurzler Brauerei who still had

---

a few notes about the recipe and interviewed Leipzigers familiar with the style. When he couldn't find a local brewery to make the beer, he turned to the Schultheiss Brauerei in what was then East Berlin to make it under contract. Gose began flowing at Ohne Bedenken in 1986, but not enough for Schultheiss to continue making the beer. Goldhahn bought his own brewery, but couldn't make a go of it and eventually turned to the Andreas Schneider brewery in Bavaria (related neither to the Schneider in Essing or Schneider & Sohn in Kelheim) to make his beer.

Today Ohne Bedenken serves Gose from the Bayerischer Bahnhof brewery as its house beer. Thomas Schneider of Andreas Schneider, apparently with a newfound love of Gose and a childhood affection for trains, headed a venture supported by the national railroad company to turn a spectacular but shuttered historic train station into a brewery. Bayerischer Bahnhof Gasthaus and Gose Brauerei began brewing in 2000, and *Gose* accounts for about 30 percent of the 1,500 hectoliters (not quite 1,300 barrels) Matthias Richter brews each year.

BAHNHOF GOSE

Original Gravity: 1.044 (11 °P)
Alcohol by Volume: 4.5%
Apparent Degree of Attenuation: 77%
IBU: 10
Malts: Wheat, Pilsener
Spices: Coriander, salt
Hops: Northern Brewer
Yeast: *Weizen* yeast from a Bavarian brewery
Primary Fermentation: Yeast pitched at 68° F (20° C), rises to 72° F (22° C), 5 to 6 days
Secondary Fermentation: 2 to 3 days warm, then 2 weeks at 34° F (1° C)
Also Noteworthy: Lactic acid bacteria added before boiling

Richter brews on a shiny 15-hectoliter, copper-clad showpiece. He includes 51 percent malted wheat in *Gose*, a bit of dark wheat giving it a yellowish color. He uses an infusion mash, with rests determined by the quality of the malt. When the malt is good he will mash-in at 136° F (58° C), raise the temperature to 144° F (62° C) for 10 to 20 minutes, then to 162° F (72° C) for saccharification and to 169° F (76° C) to mash-out. The mash lasts 2½ hours, lautering 3 hours more.

He boils the wort with lactic acid fermented in the cellar, starting with lactic acid bacteria from the surface of his malt, adding unhopped wort to it in the special fermenter. That fermentation lasts two days at 118° F (48° C), and the mixture is ready for the main wort. "We cannot use the old way, because we produce different beers in the same fermentation cellar," he said. "The lactic acid bacteria could infect the other beers."

He makes a single addition of Northern Brewer hops from Hallertau, targeting 10 IBU, along with 500 grams of salt from the pub kitchen, then a modest portion of coriander at the end. "I treat it like an aroma hop," he said.

He pitches a *weizen* yeast acquired from Bavaria, the same one he uses in his *hefeweizen,* at 68° F (20° C), allowing it to increase only to 72° F (22° C) during 5 to 6 days. Fermentation takes place in cylindro-conical tanks, which restrains the esters and phenols. "We don't want too much wheat aroma in the *Gose,*" he said. In contrast, he ferments the *hefeweizen* in an open fermenter with a self-skimming chute.

He lets the beer rest warm for 2 or 3 days after primary fermentation, cooling it to 34° F (1° C) over the course of 24 hours, then lagering it 2 weeks at the same temperature. Bahnhof sells most of its *Gose* on draft, with some bottled for sale at the pub and for export to Italy, the United States, and Denmark. The bottles contain 2.55 volumes of CO_2, while a Berliner *weisse* (brewed for export to the United States and not sold in Germany) contains 2.75 volumes. "We can't do more. It would be too difficult to fill bottles," he said. To increase the CO_2 would require bottle conditioning.

A second Gose joined Bahnhof in the Leipzig market in 2002, when a local brewery began making *Döllnitzer Ritterguts Gose* under contract for a descendant of the original owners of Rittergutsbrauerei Döllnitzer, the dominant Gose brewery of the nineteenth century. After the local brewery closed, the contract went to Brauhaus Hartmannsdorf, a brewery east of Dresden. Richter said quality and consistency have improved since the move.

Most drinkers find *Ritterguts* bolder, more sour, with more coriander and more salt flavor than the Bahnhof, which may or may not make it more genuine. You can step back into the nineteenth century at Ohne Bedenken and try them side by side. The *Gosenschenke* offers a choice of cocktails that rivals any you'll see at Berliner *weisse* specialists in Berlin, including Gose blended with raspberry or woodruff, of course, but also cherry, Curaçao, and a mixture of banana and strawberry juice. Gose mixed with a local caraway liqueur called *Allasch*, tasting of almonds, can be particularly warming on a December evening.

Bayerischer Bahnhof also features a cocktail menu. "I like it pure," Richter said. "But for many people the Gose is too sour."

When we drank Gose at Ohne Bedenken the server didn't express surprise that we ordered our beers straight. But at Sinfonie in Leipzig, a chic bistro (with an old-fashioned tavern complete with Gose memorabilia tucked off to the side) closer to the city center, our waitress suggested we might prefer a beer cocktail when we first ordered *Ritterguts*. When she delivered our beers she repeated the invitation, assuring us that asking for juice to cut the sourness would be sociably acceptable.

"Old Gose was more sour. Many times you must mix it with something sweet," Richter said, explaining why some consider *Ritterguts* more authentic. "Then the lactic acid was still living. Very hard for your stomach."

Of course, he added, many drinkers never get that far.

"People in Germany say, 'You like Gose, or you don't like Gose.' "

chapter thirteen

THE CARE AND BREWING OF RELICS

"Brewing a style you never tasted is a challenge."
– Scott Smith, East End Brewing

What seemed like an idea so full of promise one day smelled like a very bad one the next.

Scott Smith of East End Brewing in Pittsburgh and Bill Kroft of Marzoni's Brick Oven and Brewing in nearby Duncansville had one "sour mash" under their belts. That one had gone well enough at Marzoni's that they were ready to attempt brewing a Gose in Pittsburgh.

Both had concerns about bringing wild yeast into their respective breweries. Smith's best-selling beer is an India pale ale, and he had visions of ending up with a sour IPA. "A sour mash seemed liked a more conservative approach," he said. They began their two-beer collaboration by brewing a Lichtenhainer, another old style once made with wheat, using a sour mash. Rather than souring half of that mash, as they would in Smith's 10-barrel Pittsburgh brew house, they soured a modest 15 percent in a picnic cooler, then combined that with wort created using a conventional mash.

Things went a little differently in Pittsburgh. They started by mashing in half of their grist at 130 to 140° F (54 to 60° C) and letting it sit overnight. "You come into the brewery the next morning and there's a *smell*," Smith said, speaking a little more slowly. "*This smell*, best described as hot summer garbage. The most foul thing."

It filled the entire building. Smith dutifully kept it going by running off some of the liquid into the hot water reservoir of his electric keg washer to heat it, and pumping that back into the mash to stabilize the temperature at 135° F (51° C). When customers visit East End to buy growlers to go, they step pretty much right into the brew house. Heads turned.

EAST END HERE IT GOSE AGAIN
Original Gravity: 1.035 (8.8 °P)
Alcohol by Volume: 3.4%
Apparent Degree of Attenuation: 74%
IBU: 10
Malts: Pilsener, amber, flaked wheat, flaked oats
Spices: Coriander, salt
Hops: Styrian Golding
Yeast: Neutral house ale strain
Primary Fermentation: Yeast pitched at 65° F (18° C), rises to 70° F (21° C), 14 days total in fermenter before kegging
Secondary Fermentation: None—unitank, unfiltered

The smell of garbage was just as strong on Day Two. "As if you threw away a lot of lemonade," Smith said. By Day Three the smell was all lemonade, and the pH of the mash was 2.5.

Smith and Kroft proceeded with the plan to add the rest of the grist on top of what was in the mash tun and conduct another mash. When they started to run that off into the boiling kettle, they found out the smell was nothing compared to their real problem. The runoff began clear but quickly turned to milky and full of starch. The mash stuck. They spent three hours running it through a strainer bag to fill the kettle, then boiled the liquid for thirty minutes.

They ran that into the fermenter, but they weren't going to end up with beer. The pH was so low it turned off all enzymatic activity, and all they had was starch and protein. "There was no sugar to ferment," Smith said. "It was possibly the worst thing I ever brought out of the tank at the brewery. We ended up, as they say, storing it in the drain."

Another smell filled the room. "Burnt hair."

Smith looked in the empty kettle. "It was like corn chowder. It had burned a layer of it on the bottom," Smith said. He had to chip off the blackened residue by hand.

They called that beer *Here Gose Nothing*. Undeterred they tried again. This time they transferred wort from the sour mash into the brewing kettle after three days, emptied the grain out of the mash tun, then mashed the second half of the grist in a more traditional way. They ran that into the brewing kettle and boiled it all for thirty minutes to pasteurize the mixture.

They ended up with a beer called *Here It Gose Again*. This version poured stunningly clear and proved surprisingly popular. "I thought it would be a beer for geeks like me. That slightly sour flavor had a broad appeal," Smith said. Talking in the fall of 2009 Smith said he wasn't sure when he next would brew a Gose but made it clear he doesn't fear extraordinary beers. He used sixty loaves of rye bread to brew an old-style Russian beer called *Kvass*.

When he was serving *Here It Gose Again* customers had a choice of four very different wheat beers—a *wit*, a *hefeweizen* called *Monkey Boy*, the Gose, and an IPA made with wheat. "Four totally unrelated beers, the only commonality being they were all made with wheat," Smith said. " 'What is that flavor I'm getting?' That was an ongoing discussion." Each seemed to have its own "tang," perhaps because of the wheat, but the *wit* included spices, the *weizen* banana and clove flavors, the IPA hops, and the Gose sour notes.

Unlike other brewers who talk about customers matriculating from *weizens* to *wits*, Smith saw *Monkey Boy* turn his *wit* from a year-round beer into a spring seasonal. "I don't know if it was the name or the beer, but it just took off and didn't slow down," said Smith, who kept busy all summer brewing kegs sold at PNC Park, home of the Pittsburgh Pirates. "The amazing thing is that people would say, 'I don't like wheat beer but I like that.' I'm not sure what to make of it. It used to be I had to force a taster on them. Somehow they had this perception about wheat beers. Don't know if it is the bland American style . . ."

It took an entire summer for Nodding Head Brewery & Restaurant to sell its first batch of *Ich bin ein Berliner Weisse* in 2001. Now brewer Gordon Grubb makes seven batches a summer. When Phil Markowski won a gold medal at the 2002 Great American Beer Festival for Southampton Publick Houses's *Berliner Weisse* he entered it as an experimental beer, because the GABF offered no appropriate category. Now there is, and Markowski won another gold medal in 2009.

Granted the fifty barrels a year that Nodding Head sells and the once-a-year batch at Southampton wouldn't satisfy Napoleon's troops for long. However, Dogfish Head Craft Brewery describes its *Festina Pêche,* made with peaches, as "neo-Berliner *weisse.*" Were we to classify it as Berliner *weisse per se*, then it would be the second-best-selling one *in the world.*

Even with Dogfish's production factored in, today's American brewers do not come close to matching the rather modest production of nineteenth century *weiss* beer brewers. Still, Curt Decker, managing partner at Nodding Head, sees a trend. "I love the idea it is getting around. There might be twenty places in the country making it now," he said. Additionally, importer B. United International distributes two Berliner *weisse* beers brewed in Germany specifically for the American market.

ICH BIN EIN BERLINER WEISSE
Original Gravity: 1.034 (8.5 °P)
Alcohol by Volume: 3.5%
Apparent Degree of Attenuation: 79%
IBU: 5 (or less)
Malts: Wheat, Pilsener
Hops: Low alpha
Yeast: Blend of ale yeast and *Lactobacillus*
Primary Fermentation: Primary complete within 3 days; spends 5 to 6 weeks in tank

"It's such a great summer refresher," Decker said. Nodding Head dutifully offers customers the option of drinking *Ich bin ein Berliner Weisse* with juice, but as beer sales went up, syrup usage went down. "I prefer it straight," Grubb said. "I like people to try it the first time straight. This is not a complex beer like *gueuze.* When you start adding flavors, you can overwhelm it."

Grubb uses 40 percent wheat in the grist, does a single infusion and boils the wort for a brief 10 minutes. He pitches a blend of yeast for the first brew each year, then harvests from one batch to the next. Primary fermentation takes only 2 or 3 days. "If I was homebrewing I would transfer it then," he said. "I want it to be as clean as possible. Clean and tart." The first batch will condition 5 to 6 weeks until it is ready. Each successive one will go a little more quickly.

He prefers a Berliner *weisse* without *Brettanomyces* character. "I (recently) had a homebrewed batch that was fermented only with *Brett*. It was great, you didn't get any *Brett* flavor," he said. "There are different ways to skin a cat. It's what's in the glass."

Three more examples:

- Markowski first brewed *Berliner Weisse* at home in the late 1980s. "I remember trying to culture dregs from *Berliner Kindl Weisse*. I was looking for fermentation activity, and there wasn't any," he said. "It wasn't until later I learned that *Lactobacillus* doesn't act like *Saccharomyces*." He brewed several more batches as a homebrewer. "I did my first successful one in the mid-'90s. I don't remember if I purchased a culture or if something went sour," he said.

At Southampton he conducts a regular *Saccharomyces* fermentation and then inoculates the beer with *Lactobacillus*, aging it in half-barrel kegs. He allows the yeast to settle out, which takes two to three months depending on the season and temperature. He doesn't filter it or make any effort to remove the remaining *Lactobacillus* when he bottles, conditioning with fresh yeast and sucrose. He aims for 3.5 volumes of CO_2 in the bottle, producing a sodalike head.

- Dr. Fritz Briem, technology director at Doemens brewing academy, wrote the recipe for *1809*, which is brewed at Weihenstephan to export to the United States. The beer is made with 50 percent wheat and a single-step decoction. Hops are added to the mash so they isomerize during the decoction part of the mash. The wort is not boiled but only heated up to boiling temperature and then transferred to fermenters and pitched with yeast and lactic acid bacteria (isolated from malt).

Briem said he did not consider historical research when he decided to add hops in the mash. "My approach has been more, 'What have been the technical and technological abilities during that time?' and, most of all, 'What could a brewer have thought when observing his brews, the resulting beers, and especially the reaction of the people who enjoyed the product?' " he said.

- Matthias Richter brews Bayerischer Bahnhof's *Berliner's Style Weisse,* combining four brews for one 50-hectoliter batch destined for the United States. "It is not possible to sell Berliner *weisse* in Leipzig," he said. "Leipzigers drink Leipziger Gose, not Berliner *weisse.*" He mashes the beer much like his *weizen,* including a 10-minute protein rest at 122° F (45° C). He adds the same lactic acid he uses in Gose along with hops, and heats the wort to 208° F (98° C) for 30 minutes to sterilize. "We don't want to precipitate out too much of the protein," he said.

He pitches his *weizen* yeast at 68° F (20° C) and lets it rise to 79° F (26° C) in an open fermenter set apart from the other fermenters. The first 3 batches spend 1 week at 68° F (20° C), then the fourth is added to produce CO_2. He cools the beer to 34° F (1° C) for a week and bottles it, targeting 2.75 volumes of CO_2.

At first Steve Mashington of Yards Brewing Company found it nerve-wracking to brew a style of beer he had never tasted. "Then I realized nobody was going to say, 'Hey, this doesn't taste like a genuine Grodziski,' " he said, stopping to laugh.

He started thinking about brewing a Grodziski/Grätzer after reading a single paragraph in Michael Jackson's *Beer Companion.* Jackson described it as a pale golden beer, slightly hazy, with a dense white head and light body. "It has a sourish, sappy, oaky aroma (like a box that has held smoked herring), and a smoky, very dry, crisp palate," he wrote in the early 1990s, shortly before the last producer closed.

IRON YARDS LITTLE URBAN UNDERACHIEVER/SMOKED POL
Original Gravity: 1.053 (13 °P)
Alcohol by Volume: 5.6%
Apparent Degree of Attenuation: 90%
IBU: 40
Malts: Smoked barley malt, wheat malt, acidulated malt, Pilsener, melanoidin
Hops: Northern Brewer, Saaz
Yeast: WLP029 Kolsch
Primary Fermentation: 64° F (18° C) 4 days, then brought down
Secondary Fermentation: 34° F (1° C), 12 days

Mashington thought resurrecting the defunct style would make a good project for the old Yards brewing system but put it aside, because that couldn't be recommissioned until 2010. Then he mentioned the beer to Justin Sproul, brewer at Iron Hill Brewery & Restaurant in Newark, Delaware, and Sproul suggested a collaboration at the Iron Hill brewery. They made the beer to serve during Philly Beer Week 2009.

Mashington consulted with Randy Mosher, who wrote about Grätzer in *Radical Brewing*, to formulate the recipe. Grätzer/Grodziski was traditionally brewed with smoked wheat malt, but Yards/Iron Hill needed 500 pounds, and the only option would have been to smoke it themselves. No commercial maltster sells smoked wheat malt, and recall that the two Bamberg breweries still producing their own smoked malt use unsmoked wheat in their smoked wheat beers. The practical recipe called for smoked barley malt and wheat malt.

"I'd love to use smoked wheat malt," said Mashington, talking about the possibility of making the beer a regular seasonal offering at Yards to honor the memory of Thaddeus Kosciuszko, the Polish-born general who was a hero in the American Revolution.

Little Urban Underachiever turned out to be more drinkable than he expected. "It had the body of the wheat beer and a little smokiness, a little tartness," he said. "It wasn't nearly as smoky (as *Schlenkerla Rauchweizen*), just enough to intrigue but not enough to turn off somebody who didn't like smoked beers."

The past yields many brewing surprises.

chapter fourteen

FOUR RESURRECTED RECIPES

"These were the first beers that I had that didn't really taste like beer to me. At the time I thought they were all very good but didn't understand how special and regional they were."

– Kristen England, homebrewer

How sour was Lichtenhainer?

How salty was Gose?

How smoky and how bitter was Grätzer?

Sometimes Kristen England had to do a bit of guessing when he came up with the recipes for such beers, but taste bud-opening adventures in northern Germany provided more than a few clues. He drank Berliner *weisse* in Berlin, Gose in Leipzig, and Lichtenhainer in Wöllnitz.

He has only had Grätzer at home.

Researching styles no longer brewed or barely brewed suits him fine. He was a Ph.D. candidate at the University of Minnesota when he started homebrewing in 2003, and he approached it like a scientist, if somewhat maniacally, keeping diligent notes "with angry questions marks all over the tasting notes." Within a few years he had won four cases' worth of brewing medals, become the youngest BJCP Grand Master judge ever, earned his doctorate in pharmacology, and celebrated by heading to Eastern and Central Europe to visit relatives and drink more beer.

Kristen England shares a drink with his wife's great-uncle, Rafael, in Pusztaföldvár, Hungary. (Photo courtesy of Kristen England.)

"I do research for a living, so I know what it takes to find the actual answer," he said. Because he is a decent reader of German, he expected using technical texts would be easy. "At least I thought that until I started reading brewing texts," he said. "They have their own vernacular, and I had to get a turn-of-the-century, German-English brewing dictionary, no kidding." These provided him not only exact measures ("How many Bavarian *Eimers* are in a hectoliter again?) for making a Berliner *weisse* but "more importantly, how one should taste."

He acquired the thirst when he lived in Sweden for a year as a student at Michigan State University. He did more traveling than studying, drinking a variety of beers along the way. "I was used to drinking 'regular' beer, and by regular I mean 'not funky,' " he said. A waitress in Berlin talked him into, among many other things, trying *Schultheiss Berliner Weisse*. She gave him a history of the region, including both Gose and Lichtenhainer. Soon he was off to Leipzig and Wöllnitz, to be disappointed by the *Bayerischer Bahnhof Gose*—because, most agree, the original would have been much sourer—but delighted by Lichtenhainer. "This is something that I completely loved and didn't realize it was a style unto itself until after I drank it," he said. "I thought it was a wonderful, sour little wheat beer with a touch of smoke."

Grätzer (or Grodziskie or Grodiski) was more of a challenge, given that the last version was brewed in Poland in the 1990s. His interest began when he read a passage in the *American Handy Book of the Brewing, Malting, and Auxiliary Trades,* and his curiosity about why a beer style could be so popular and then disappear fueled it further. He suspects it was because of the anti-Polish mentality of the Germans during its decline. Reading about the beer in both Polish and German sources, he found recipes listing different levels of bitterness, amounts of wheat, various percentages of smoked malt, types of wood for smoking the malt, and copious amounts of other conflicting information about any other variable worth considering.

He wrote the recipe after numerous emails with Ron Pattinson, who has called Grätzer one of his personal obsessions. Of all the eclectic German wheat styles, it turned out to be England's favorite. "I went in to the thing thinking, ah, 'This is gonna suck something fierce. Smoke and bitterness? There is a reason why the Bambergers don't hop their beers strongly, and this has a ton of hops in it,' " he said. "Not to mention, what nutbar would use 100 percent wheat malt?"

Three months after he brewed and bottled the beer, he had pretty much forgotten about it, when he literally stumbled across two cases in his St. Paul cellar. "Since I was already three fingers deep into a bottle of Lagavulin, I didn't think I would be able to taste much," he said. "Pow! Even through the succulent peat reek from my Scotch glass the smoke and bitterness came roaring through. This is one of those rare moments when I was speechless . . . and that's saying something."

England begins talking faster and using more exclamation points when discussing his favorite brewing subjects. He's convinced that most research underestimates the character of some defunct beers. "Case in point, the amount of smoke and hop in this very low-gravity beer is absolutely massive," he said. "Today's self-proclaimed 'beer experts' love the imperial-triple-bourbon-barrel-iced-*Brettanomyces*-barley wine types of beers . . . if they had one of these the way it was supposed to be made, their collective 'sheeple' minds would explode."

He first brewed a Berliner *weisse* in 2005. The other three seemed to follow naturally. When he sent the Berliner *weisse* recipe for this book he wrote, "Like all German beers, it's quite simple." Yes and no. Instructions on conducting a decoction mash or how to grow up the large portion of *Lactobacillus* yeast (starters from Wyeast or White Labs work equally well) are beyond the scope of this book.

He emphasizes the importance of using a neutral German or European ale yeast rather than a *weizen* strain. He experimented with a *weizen* yeast in the Lichtenhainer, and as much as he enjoys bananas and bacon, he discovered those flavors don't work together in beer.

All but the Grätzer should have a good amount of sourness coming out of primary but won't reach top sourness until about six months. "The sooner you get this into the bottle, the better," England said. "Like in the old days, when it would go out to the landlord right after it was brewed." It must be highly carbonated, so using thick-walled bottles is essential.

"The final beer should be very effervescent, and if done correctly have apple and pear notes with touches of bread dough in the nose," he said. "The flavor should have a mouthfilling, biscuity, wheat flavor and a crisp, dry, tart finish. These can range from having a touch of sourness to *very* sour. Most importantly, a Berliner *weisse* should be crystal clear. Importantly, you have a lot of lame-o fakers out there, so a very easy way to tell if someone added lactic acid to their Berliner is the flavor. Lactic acid will lend a sharper bitterness and a salty-type quality to the beer. Lactate, produced by the lacto in a true Berliner, even though very sour, will seem rounder and won't have that 'salty' character."

Traditional Berliner Weisse
Original Gravity: 1.034 (8.5 °P)
Final Gravity: 1.008 (2 °P)
Alcohol by Volume: ~3%
IBU: 5

Grain Bill:
Pilsener 50%
Wheat 50%

Mashing:
Add hops to mash during decoction boil
Single decoction
Mash in at 133° F (56° C) for 1 hour
Raise temperature to 152° F (67° C) for 15 minutes
Pull decoction and boil for 20 minutes
Return to raise the temperature to 166° F (74° C), rest 30 minutes

Hops: Any German (5 IBU)

Boiling: None

Yeast: *Lactobacillus* and a neutral German or European ale yeast at a ratio of 5:1

Fermentation: 70-75° F (21-24° C). Cool fermentation will reduce the amount of sourness and final *Lacto* numbers. Should be complete after 3 days. No secondary.

Bottling: Bottle with kraeusen to 4 volumes, re-yeasting with 10,000 cells per milliliter. Condition the bottles at 75° F (24° C) for a few weeks.

Lichtenhainer

Although this beer is very similar in character to a Berliner *weisse*, smoke changes it immensely. "The luscious, bacony, beechwood-smoked Bamberg malt adds a true 'hammy' quality to this beer but doesn't overpower the doughy wheat," England said. "I find that going over 40 percent smoked malt in this beer pushes the beer too far into the 'deli section' of the beer market and makes it quite flabby tasting. Pun intended." The beer should not taste as sour as a Berliner *weisse*.

Original Gravity: 1.046 (11.5 °P)
Final Gravity: 1.008 (2 °P)
Alcohol by Volume: 4.8%
IBU: 10

Grain Bill:
Wheat malt 37.5%
Beechwood-smoked malt 37.5%
Pilsener 25%

Mashing:
Single decoction
Mash-in at 133° F (56° C) for 1 hour
Raise temperature to 152° F (67° C) for 15 minutes
Pull decoction and boil for 20 minutes
Return to raise the temperature to 166° F (74° C), rest 30 minutes

Hops: Spalt, first wort (12 IBU)

Boiling: 90 minutes

Yeast: *Lactobacillus* and a neutral German or European ale yeast at a ratio of 2.5 to 3:1

Fermentation: 70-75° F (21-24° C). Cool fermentation will reduce the amount of sourness and final *Lacto* numbers. Should be complete after 3 days. No secondary.

Bottling: Bottle with kraeusen to 4 volumes, re-yeasting with 10,000 cells per milliliter. Condition the bottles at 75° F (24° C) for a few weeks.

Gose

The Gose includes small changes in the grist from the Berliner *weisse* plus the addition of salt and coriander. "This beer should be at least as sour, if not more, as a Berliner," England said. "Because of the Munich malt and salt added it should remind you of a lunch of crusty bread eaten beside the ocean. The thing I find most wrong with the Gose recreations is that people put way too much coriander and not enough salt. I still haven't had one yet with enough sourness."

Original Gravity: 1.046 (11.5 °P)
Final Gravity: 1.008 (2 °P)
Alcohol by Volume: 4.8%
IBU: 10

Grain Bill:
Wheat malt 58%
Munich 21%
Pilsener 21%

Mashing: 151° F (66° C) for 90 minutes

Hops: Perle and/or Hallertauer, 90 minutes (11 IBU)

Spices:
0.13 ounces coriander per gallon (1g/L), added the last 10 minutes
12.4 grams salt per gallon (3.3g/L), added at knockout

Boiling: 90 minutes

Yeast: *Lactobacillus* and a neutral German or European ale yeast at a ratio of 5:1

Fermentation: 70-75° F (21-24° C). Cool fermentation will reduce the amount of sourness and final *Lacto* numbers. Ferment in the primary for about a week and about another week in the secondary.

Bottling: Bottle with kraeusen to 4 volumes, re-yeasting with 10,000 cells per milliliter. Condition the bottles at 75° F (24° C) for a few weeks.

Grätzer

This beer, which is not sour, takes more time and extra effort plus the equipment to smoke the malt. Instructions can be found in *Smoked Beers* by Ray Daniels and Geoff Larson. "Of all the beers here, find a way to do this one," England said.

"You could substitute Bamberg smoked malt, but then you wouldn't be using 100 percent wheat, and the beechwood is too soft and lacks the sharpness of oak," he said. "Be sure to get white oak, as it is much less sweet than the red variety. If done right, this beer will be exceedingly dry and very bitter. The astringency is what gets me with this one. All the tannins from the hops and phenols from the smoke work in concert with the sweet, doughy wheat malt. Unity in duality as it were. The first time I opened one of these for some friends, the guys across the room smelled the smoke reek instantly."

Original Gravity: 1.028 (7 °P)
Final Gravity: 1.012 (3 °P)
Alcohol by Volume: 3.1%
IBU: 32

Grain Bill:
Wheat malt 100%, home smoked with oak
1 pound rice hulls added during lauter

Mashing:
122° F (50° C) for 30 minutes
149° F (65° C) for 90 minutes

Hops:
German Northern Brewer, first wort (29 IBU)
Hallertau, 15 minutes (3 IBU)

Boiling: 90 minutes

Yeast: Neutral German or European ale yeast

Fermentation: 70-75° F (21-24° C). A week in the primary and a week in the secondary (optional).

Bottling: Bottle with kraeusen to 4 volumes, re-yeasting with 10,000 cells per milliliter. Condition the bottles at 75° F (24° C) for a few weeks.

PART VI:
PUTTING IT ALL TOGETHER

chapter fifteen
BETTER BREWING, JUDGING, AND ENJOYING

"When I had Allagash (White) *I was really impressed with the 'Triple Sec'-like aromas and high attenuation. I bought* Flying Dog Woody Creek White *last week, and it was very complex and highly carbonated! Both are proof that Americans can produce better* witbiers *than many Belgians."*

– Derek Walsh, international beer judge, the Netherlands

Steven Pauwels grabbed the computer mouse and, click, opened a folder showing the recipes for Boulevard Brewing. He clicked again and the spreadsheet on the large computer screen in front of us revealed the recipe for *Unfiltered Wheat Beer* in detail, as well as the process. *Click* again, and the screen displayed a brew house schematic for a batch of *Single Wide IPA* in progress. Next, he opened a spreadsheet with a recipe for ZÔN, Boulevard's seasonal *wit*. "Copy whatever you want," he said.

The conversation turned to mashing schedules and a presentation Hans-Peter Drexler had made at the 2008 Craft Brewers Conference in San Diego, revealing "the secrets" about how Private Weissbierbrauerei G. Schneider & Sohn makes its iconic *Schneider Weisse Original*. "Hans-Peter is so open, he could be American," Pauwels said.

Here was a Belgian who moved to Kansas City in 1999, talking about a German and himself and sharing every detail of how Boulevard brews its beers. Pardon me for smiling.

When I returned from visiting Belgium and Germany, homebrewers would ask what secrets I had discovered, perhaps expecting I would mention something about a secret spice for *wit*. In fact, I'm not sure I learned any secrets, but as you have seen on the previous pages an awful lot of brewers let me look over their shoulders, explained exactly what they were doing and why. For some readers this is pleasure enough. Others will want to take the knowledge and put it to practical use.

As I wrote at the outset, "wheat" does not constitute a style. However, style guidelines and some real-world examples may help you jump start whatever action you take next. While I was writing this book, many visitors to www.brewingwithwheat.com offered outstanding questions and tips about evaluating "to style," and those often ended up incorporated in previous chapters. However, as in *Brew Like a Monk,* a single voice sometimes rings clearer, so I asked Gordon Strong for input on what both brewers and judges should know about the styles and guidelines. He is president of the Beer Judge Certification Program, wrote large parts of the group's guidelines, and twice won the Ninkasi Award in the National Homebrew Competition, given to the brewer who scores the most points for awards in the final round. Additionally, his *hefeweizen* won gold in the 2009 NHC. He bases his comments on BJCP guidelines, but I find they ring true whether you are drinking for pleasure or brewing "to style."

Some beers mentioned in the previous pages don't fit in style guidelines, particularly those in Parts IV and V. I have included the specifications from both the BJCP guidelines and from the Brewers Association Beer Style Guidelines, which are used for judging at the Great American Beer Festival and World Beer Cup, allowing you to compare them with information about examples of those styles. The descriptions that go with the guidelines make both more meaningful, and I suggest reading them in full. The BJCP guidelines may be found at www.bjcp.org, the BA Beer Styles at www.brewersassociation.org.

Belgian White/Wit

	Original Gravity SG (Plato)	Alcohol by Volume	Apparent Extract (FG)	Color SRM (EBC)	Bitterness (IBU)
BJCP	1.044-1.052 (11-12.9 °P)	4.5-5.5%	1.008-1.012 (2-3 °P)	2-4	10-20
Brewers Association	1.044-1.050 (11-12.5 °P)	3.8-4.4%	1.006-1.010 (1.5-2.5 °P)	2-4 (4-8)	10-17
Hoegaarden White	1.049 (12.2 °P)	5.1%	1.012 (3 °P)	3 (6)	14
Allagash White	1.048 (12 °P)	5%	1.010 (2.5 °P)	3 (6)	21
Wittekerke	1.046 (11.5 °P)	4.7	1.011 (2.7 °P)	3.5 (7)	11
Celis White (Van Steenberge)	1.047 (11.7 °P)	4.8%	1.010 (2.5 °P)	3 (6)	9
Gulpener Korenwolf	1.047 (11.6 °P)	4.9%	1.009 (2.3 °P)	3.75 (7.5)	14
Jan De Lichte	1.063 (15.4 °P)	7.3%	1.008 (2 °P)	4.5 (9)	18

Data courtesy of Derek Walsh and breweries

Mashing and lautering: The danger of a stuck mash is not as great as with a beer that contains a higher percentage of wheat, but one-half cup of rice hulls in a 5-gallon batch adds a bit of insurance. Mashing out at 172° F (78° C) will also promote a smooth runoff. Although most Belgian wheat yeast strains don't contain as strong a precursor for production of 4-vinyl guaiacol as *weizen* yeast, you will still benefit from mashing-in higher than 117° F (47° C) if you want to avoid clove character. A rest at 122° F (50° C) will promote cloudiness.

Brewing with extract: Steeping with unmalted grains will not add any sugar for fermentation, so plan your recipe accordingly. To provide starch haze add 1 tablespoon of flour to the boil (may also benefit all-grain brewers).

Balancing tartness and spices: Most brewers feel today's *wit* beer yeasts create an appropriate level of tartness. To get more, consider using acidulated malt in the grist or food-grade lactic acid.

Recall that earlier Steven Pauwels of Boulevard Brewing said, "I like the idea of tartness in white beers. Nowadays we tend to over-spice these beers to reach that goal, while they were pretty simple beers at that time." His *wit* won a gold medal at the Great American Beer Festival. He suggests that homebrewers limit themselves to 1 gram of both orange peel and coriander per gallon, which amounts to just about one-sixth of 1 ounce each for a 5-gallon batch. That equates to 27 grams per hectoliter, which, in fact, is the amount of orange peel Boulevard uses in its *wit*. Pauwels has cut the coriander dose to 16 grams per hectoliter, explaining, "It is easier to over-spice a beer than to find a balance."

In Belgium By Beer, Beer By Belgium the authors report that at the turn of the century, brewers in the Leuven region included 50 grams each of orange peel and coriander per hectoliter. Jean-François Gravel's recipe in Chapter 5 calls for considerably more coriander (comparable to 75 to 125 grams per hectoliter) and 50 grams per hectoliter of orange peel. The 1 ounce per barrel of coriander that Derek Osborne of BJ's Restaurants adds to his award-winning *Nit Wit* translates to about 25 grams per hectoliter. He adds the same amounts of sweet and bitter orange peel.

Derek Walsh, who provided the data for most of these charts, points out that several breweries began producing "*Dubbel-wit*" in the 1990s. He particularly likes De Glazen Toren *Jan De Lichte* "for its sweet, oily, spicy, hoppy balance" and more-than-average hop dosage. He judges in many international competitions, including World Beer Cup and the Great American Beer Festival. "Judging *witbier* is not one of my favorite pastimes. It's often too sweet due to low attenuation and/or carbonation and misses spice balance and complexity due to one-dimensional use of old spices," he said. "Judges often don't get the idea that it needs to be dry and refreshing and not a cloyingly sweet herbal concoction."

Gordon Strong: Flaws and Misconceptions
- Making it too bitter. Overspicing it. Spices are taking the place of late hops; they should be balanced.
- Too thick/heavy. It's supposed to be a refreshing beer and easy to drink. Extra malt flavors. This is basically a *pils* malt and wheat beer; other malt flavors are unwelcome.
- Not serving it fresh enough. Most wheat beers don't store well.
- Not handling the spices properly or using a poor quality of spices. It shouldn't taste soapy or like celery seed or ham.

What should judges better understand?

- It's a delicate style. Less is more. Brash, bold spice bombs are not authentic. The overall impression should be light and refreshing.
- Look for freshness; a light, refreshing body and finish; high carbonation; a clean malt/wheat flavor; subdued bitterness; balanced, clean spice flavors. A fresh yeast character and lack of fermentation faults.
- The malt/wheat flavor should carry the beer, with the spices adding interest. The bitterness should be sufficient to keep it from being sweet but shouldn't be noticeable. Hops shouldn't get in the way of spices.
- The yeast character can have some interest but isn't as aggressive as some Belgian styles. It shouldn't have too much acidity.
- The appearance is important; the color should be very pale, with a big, pure-white head. A hazy shine is desired.

German Weizen Beers

	Original Gravity SG (Plato)	Alcohol by Volume	Apparent Extract (FG)	Color SRM (EBC)	Bitterness (IBU)
BJCP	1.044-1.052 (11-12.9 °P)	4.3-5.6%	1.010-1.014 (2.5-3.5 °P)	2-8 (4-16)	8-15
BA *Hefeweizen*	1.047-1.056 (11.8-14 °P)	4.9-5.5%	1.008-1.016 (2-4 °P)	3-9 (6-18)	10-15
BA *Bernsteinfarbenes*	1.048-1.056 (12-14 °P)	4.8-5.4%	1.008-1.016 (2-4 °P)	18-26 (9-13)	10-15
Erdinger Hefe-Weizen	1.050 (12.4 °P)	5.4%	1.008 (2 °P)	5 (10)	16
Schneider Weisse Original	1.052 (12.8 °P)	5.4%	1.011 (2.8 °P)	10.5 (21)	12
Spaten Hefeweissbier	1.047 (11.7 °P)	5%	1.009 (2.3 °P)	7 (14)	12
Paulaner Hefe-Weissbier	1.051 (12.5 °P)	5.5%	1.009 (2.5 °P)	8 (16)	13

Data courtesy of Derek Walsh and breweries

Water: Brewing water throughout Bavaria varies widely. Munich water total hardness measures 265 parts per million and calcium hardness 190 ppm, while other German *weizen* brewers use water with one-third that hardness. Basically, what works for your other beers should work for *weizen*.

Mashing and lautering: Take the same measures as you would with Belgian wheat beers, but remember that a rest at 109 to 113° F (43 to 45° C) promotes production of ferulic acid and can add the appropriate clove flavors to your beer.

Brewing with extract: Extract is an excellent alternative for a brewer whose system won't accommodate a ferulic acid rest. For instance, Briess extract includes 65 percent wheat and might be called "4-vinyl guaiacol-ready." Before Bob Hansen became manager of technical services at Briess Malt & Ingredients Company, he brewed at Water Street Brewing in Milwaukee, a brewpub that made beer from extract rather than malted barley and wheat. In 2000 his *Raspberry Weiss* won a silver medal at the Great American Beer Festival. His Bavarian *hefeweizen* regularly accounted for more than one-third of pub sales.

A bit of color: Two BA guidelines, which mirror those used in other international competitions, are listed here, mostly to account for difference in color. The BA guidelines also include Krystalweizen (filtered) and Leichtes Weizen (lighter because of a lower starting gravity). BJCP guidelines designate Hefeweizen as the only style lighter than Dunkelweizen. All of this is a reminder that *hefeweizens* need not be totally pale.

"It should have some caramel and Munich," said Jonathan Cutler of Piece Brewery & Pizzeria. "There should be some malt sweetness." Andreas Richter at Weyermann Malting said all the larger breweries in Germany include caramel malt in their recipes. "It will complement the esters," he said.

The Big D: Research at Weissbierbrauerei G. Schneider & Sohn has found that with protein higher than 13 percent and the Kolbach index above 45 percent, diacetyl becomes a larger problem. In simplest terms be sure to conduct a proper diacetyl rest. Additionally, be aware that bottle conditioning with a second yeast will create diacetyl, so condition for a proper period.

Dunkelweizen

	Original Gravity SG (Plato)	Alcohol by Volume	Apparent Extract (FG)	Color SRM (EBC)	Bitterness (IBU)
BJCP	1.044-1.056 (11-14 °P)	4.3-5.6%	1.010-1.014 (2.5-4 °P)	14-23 (28-46)	10-18
Brewers Association	1.048-1.056 (12-14 °P)	4.8-5.4%	1.008-1.016 (2-4 °P)	10-19 (20-38)	10-15
Andechs Dunkels Weissbier	1.047 (11.7 °P)	4.9%	1.009 (2.3 °P)	25.5 (51)	13
Weihenstephaner Hefeweissbier Dunkel	1.051 (12.7 °P)	5.3%	1.010 (2.5 °P)	22 (44)	14
Spaten Hefeweissbier Dunkel	1.047 (11.7 °P)	4.9%	1.009 (2.3 °P)	17 (34)	12
Paulaner Hefe-Weissbier Dunkel	1.050 (12.4 °P)	5.4%	1.010 (2.5 °P)	14.5 (29)	13

Data courtesy of Derek Walsh and breweries

A bit of color: Weyermann suggests its Carawheat for *dunkelweizen,* adding color as well as flavor. Is there a difference between colored wheat malts and colored barley malts such as caramel, chocolate, and Victory?

"It is different in the chew. And in the wort," Hansen said. "I struggle to find a reason other than its 'Wheaties' flavor."

Richter said customers use Carawheat in festival wheat beers, *dunkelweizens,* and even *weizenbocks.*

Weizenbock

	Original Gravity SG (Plato)	Alcohol by Volume	Apparent Extract (FG)	Color SRM (EBC)	Bitterness (IBU)
BJCP	1.064-1.090 (15.7-21.6 °P)	6.5-8%	1.015-1.022 (3.8-5.6 °P)	12-25 (24-50)	15-30
Brewers Association	1.066-1.080 (16-19.5 °P)	6.9-9.3%	1.016-1.028 (4-7 °P)	4.5-30 (9-60)	15-25
Schneider Aventinus	1.076 (18.5 °P)	8.2%	1.013 (3.3 °P)	22.5 (45)	15
Erdinger Pikantus	1.065 (16.8 °P)	7.2%	1.010 (2.6 °P)	39 (78)	13
Gutmann Weizenbock	1.070 (17 °P)	7.1%	1.016 (4.1 °P)	6.5 (13)	12
Weihenstephaner Vitus	1.068 (16.5 °P)	7.7%	1.009 (2.3 °P)	6 (12)	17

Data courtesy of Derek Walsh and breweries

Fermentation: Higher original gravity produces more esters, while a lower temperature will restrain esters and promote the perception of phenols.

A bit of color: Weyermann offers a chocolate roasted wheat malt as well as chocolate malt. Richter said it adds breadlike flavors to a beer. In fact, Weyermann sells both its Carawheat and chocolate wheat to the baking industry.

"I would use the chocolate, just for the kick of it," Hansen said.

Gordon Strong: Flaws and Misconceptions

- Too bitter. *Hefeweizens* shouldn't have a noticeable bitterness. If you can taste bitterness (and hop flavor, for that matter), too many hops have been used.
- Too heavy. *Hefeweizens* should be refreshing. A heavy beer is hard to drink, so the body should be no higher than medium-light.
- Fermenting too warm often creates bubblegum flavors and sometimes funky, unclean flavors.
- Not fresh enough. *Hefeweizens* are notorious for going downhill quickly; drink them when they are young.
- Not enough carbonation. An effervescent character is an important part of the style; the beer will seem heavy and lifeless without it.

- Wrong malt profile. The wheat really should be noticeable. Lame yeast character. The banana and clove character is very distinctive. If it's not there, it won't seem like a *hefeweizen*.
- For *dunkelweizen* and *weizenbock*, it's mostly in the malt character, the balance, and the esters. The malt should be caramelly and rich, not roasty. *Dunkelweizen* can have some additional grain-derived esters, but *weizenbock* really needs them.
- For *weizenbock*, it's alcohol. Sometimes the alcohol winds up being too strong or hot. It needs to be warming and sneaky.

What should judges better understand?

- Bubblegum isn't a positive. Banana is what you want, not banana plus strawberry (which is what bubblegum tastes like).
- A range of yeast character is possible in the style; the banana and clove can vary in intensity. Bubblegum is usually a problem, but vanilla enhances the banana.
- Balance. The wheat should be noted, and the bitterness should not be apparent. The yeast character should not overwhelm the beer.
- Clean flavors are desirable. Fermenting too warm doesn't just enhance esters, it seems to cause all sorts of odd flavors.
- Yeast character is substituting for hops; the hops shouldn't be noticeable in flavor, aroma, or bitterness.
- Flavors get muted and stale when the beer gets old, and acidity often increases.
- For *dunkelweizen* and *weizenbock*, look for additional flavors that enhance and round out the beer. The beers become more complex, so there are more components to balance.

American Wheat

	Original Gravity SG (Plato)	Alcohol by Volume	Apparent Extract (FG)	Color SRM (EBC)	Bitterness (IBU)
BJCP	1.040-1.055 (10-13.6 °P)	4-5.5%	1.008-1.013 (2-3.3 °P)	3-6 (6-12)	15-30

*The category includes rye as an ingredient

Quite honestly, few of the American wheat beers presented in this book fit well into current style categories. The Brewers Association guidelines include four categories for American Wheat Ale or Lager as well as English-Style Summer Ale, so I will not list them all. Both the BJCP guidelines and the BA emphasize that German wheat character is not appropriate.

Gordon Strong: Flaws and Misconceptions

- Not understanding style is quite broad, which gives the brewer a great deal of flexibility. The balance can be hoppy or malty, the finish can be full or dry, it can have a late hop character or not—all of these are equally valid.
- Most people should know that you use a neutral American yeast in this style, but some people still get it wrong. Don't use a German *weizen* yeast.
- Not enough wheat character. It's a wheat beer, so it should have wheat flavor.

What should judges better understand?

- That the style has a broad range, and that many variations are acceptable. Avoid the halo effect of looking for a clone of one particular beer.
- The biggest range is in hop character and bitterness.
- Wheat character is a must, but the remaining balance of the beer is wide open. The beer should be judged on the overall balance: Is it pleasant? It's hard to get a beer that's out of style for this category if it contains wheat and American ingredients.

Berliner Weisse

	Original Gravity SG (Plato)	Alcohol by Volume	Apparent Extract (FG)	Color SRM (EBC)	Bitterness (IBU)
BJCP	1.028-1.032 (7-8 °P)	2.8-3.8%	1.003-1.006 (1-1.5 °P)	2-3 (4-6)	3-8
Brewers Association	1.028-1.032 (7-8 °P)	2.8-3.4%	1.004-1.006 (1-1.5 °P)	2-4 (4-8)	3-6
Schultheiss Weisse*	1.029 (7.3 °P)	3.6%	1.002 (.5 °P)	2.5 (5)	3
Berliner Kindl Weisse	1.031 (7.8 °P)	3%	1.008 (2 °P)	2.5 (5)	4

Data courtesy of Derek Walsh and breweries
*No longer brewed

The pH of the *Schultheiss Weisse* measured 3, the *Berliner Kindl Weisse* 3.2.

In his *Pocket Guide to Beer* (1984) Michael Jackson gave *Kindl Weisse* five stars and *Schultheiss Weisse* four, but later in the *Beer Companion* singled out the *Schultheiss* as a good candidate for cellaring because of bottle conditioning. Although the combined Berliner-Kindl-Schultheiss brewery discontinued *Schultheiss Weisse* production in 2006, bottles should remain available in Berlin for several more years. Jackson also wrote that upon visiting the Schultheiss brewery in the early 1990s he was told the quality control lab experimented with selecting the yeast strains. "We stopped counting after seven or eight, and fermentations with selected yeast did not produce a better beer." His words serve as a reminder that production of Berliner *weisse* always varied from brewery to brewery.

Gordon Strong: Flaws and Misconceptions

- Too big. Berliner *weisse* is a *shankbier,* so it needs to be light in alcohol by volume. A big beer will have too big a mouthfeel.
- A clean, lactic sourness is required. The sourness needs to be a dominant flavor, but it needs to be the right kind of sourness. The yeast character should be neutral, with the sourness coming from lactic acid.
- Too bitter. This beer style shouldn't be bitter at all.
- Lacking bread dough flavors. The wheat and malt flavor generally has a flavor of uncooked bread dough; it's quite distinctive.
- Not carbonated enough. Champagne-like carbonation is vital.

What should judges better understand?

- The flavor of the malt character. Any raw, bready flavors are desirable. Bread dough is the best description.
- The type and level of sourness. Sourness needs to be noticeable, not in the background. The sourness should be clean but with some complexity.
- All the flavors should be very clean. The malt and yeast character should be clean. Hops aren't noticeable.
- High carbonation is an absolute requirement; it has to be super-refreshing. Think of drinking it on a very hot day.

Gose

	Original Gravity SG (Plato)	Alcohol by Volume	Apparent Extract (FG)	Color SRM (EBC)	Bitterness (IBU)
Brewers Association	1.036-1.056 (9-14 °P)	4.4-5.4%	1.008-1.012 (2-3 °P)	3-9 (6-18)	10-15
Bayerischer Bahnhof	1.044 (11 °P)	4.5%	1.010 (2.5 °P)	5.5 (11)	10
Döllnitzer Ritterguts (2003)*	1.048 (12 °P)	4.6%	1.013 (3 °P)	6.5 (13)	9

Data courtesy of Derek Walsh and breweries
*From previous contract brewer

The pH of the *Bayerischer Bahnhof Gose* measured 3.6, the *Döllnitzer Ritterguts* 3.7.

BJCP guidelines do not currently include Gose. The Brewers Association description emphasizes traditional spontaneous fermentation, while acknowledging modern brewers don't follow the practice: "Gose is typically pale gold to pale amber in color and typically contains malted barley, unmalted wheat, with some traditional varieties containing oats. Hop character and malt flavors and aromas are negligible. Lemony or other citruslike qualities are often present in aroma and on the palate. Some versions may have the spicy character of added coriander in aroma and on the palate at low to medium levels. Salt (table salt) character is also traditional in low amounts."

Bayerischer Bahnhof Gose pours with a billowing head that, unlike the Champagne-like foam atop a Berliner *weisse*, lingers. We expect that from a wheat beer. In *German Wheat Beer* Eric Warner describes two different methods of pouring a *weissbier* (or *hefeweiss*). He prefers the "Master Pour," writing: "Hold the bottle in the dominant hand and the glass in the other hand. Tip the bottle as far as possible without letting any beer flow out, then tip the glass slightly downward and bring it over the mouth of the tilted bottle. Now slowly tilt the glass upright and begin decanting the beer slowly down the side of the glass with the mouth of the bottle as far down as possible, without ever letting it come in contact with the beer or foam. When done properly, there would be little foam on the surface of the beer. Once the glass is almost full, the bottle can be raised a couple of inches from the rim, and the remaining beer can be poured more vigorously to raise the head."

He adds that to extract more of the yeast from the bottom, empty the bottle down to the last half-inch of beer, then stop and swirl it to loosen any sediment before finishing the pour. Perhaps that's best for the integrity of the beer, but some of us are suckers for what Warner calls the "Flashy Nightclub Bartender's Pour":

"Place the *weissbier* glass upside down on top of the bottle. The glass should go about halfway before it is stopped. Quickly turn the glass and bottle over so the glass is now right side up and the bottle is upside down. The beer will rapidly pour out of the bottle until the mouth of the bottle is submerged. Then slowly pull the bottle out of the glass, keeping the mouth of the bottle beneath the surface of the beer until the bottle is empty. It is important that the mouth of the bottle stay beneath the surface of the beer, not just the foam, otherwise the beer will foam out of the glass."

Prosit.

appendix

YEAST CHARTS

White Labs Wheat Strains

			Weizen	American Wheat	Bavarian Weizen	Hefewei-zen IV	Belgian Wit
			300	320	351	380	400
Attenuation			72-76%	70-75%	73-77%	73-80%	74-78%
Flocculation			Low	Low	Low	Very Low	Low-Medium
Temp Range and Resulting Flavor Profiles		75-85	More Banana Scent	More Sulfur	High Clove, Phenolic Overtones	Clove with Citrus and Apricot	Fruity Tangy Spicy
		65-75	*Preferred for Clove Phenolics	Slight Banana, Low Clove, Hazy, Clean Fermenting	*Preferred for Clove and Spice	Clove with Citrus and Apricot	*Preferred Slightly Phenolic and Tart
		58-66	Slight Banana Clove Scent	Clean Fermenting Yeast	Crisp	Crisp	Mild with Sulfur
Alc Tolerance			Medium	Medium	Medium	Medium	Medium
Compatible Styles	Weizen/ Weissbier		✓		✓	✓	
	Dunkelweizen		✓		✓		
	Weizenbock		✓		✓	✓	
	Witbier		✓	✓	✓	✓	✓
	German Wheat		✓		✓	✓	
	American Wheat			✓			
	Berliner Weisse						
	Trippel/ Dubbel/ Strong						

White Labs Wheat Strains

			Belgian *Wit* II	Trappist	Belgian	Berliner
			410	500	550	677 Lacto
Attenuation			70-75%	75-80%	78-85%	85-89%
Flocculation			Low-Medium	Medium	Medium	Low
Temp Range and Resulting Flavor Profiles		75-85	Spicy and Sweet	Fruity, Tangy, Mild Banana	Phenols, Low Fruit, Strongly Belgian	* *Preferred* Temperature Sour, Tart
		65-75	*Preferred Temperature Low Phenol, Spicy	*Preferred, Woody, Fruity	Phenols, Spicy, Low Fruit	Lower Production of Lactic Acid, Less Sour
		58-66	Low Phenol, Spicy	Earthy, Cloves	Herbal	Too Cold
Alc Tolerance			Medium	High	High	High
Compatible Styles	*Weizen/ Weissbier*					
	Dunkelweizen					
	Weizenbock					
	Witbier		✓	✓	✓	
	German Wheat					
	American Wheat					
	Berliner *Weisse*					✓
	Trippel/Dubbel/ Strong			✓	✓	

Wyeast Laboratories Wheat Strains

Wyeast Strain Number		1007	1010	1214	2565	3056
Wyeast Strain Name		German Ale	American Wheat	Belgian Abbey	*Kölsch*	Bavarian Wheat Blend
Flocculation		Low	Low	Med-Low	Low	Medium
Attenuation %		73-77	74-78	74-78	73-77	73-77
Alcohol Tolerance % by Weight		11	10	12	10	10
Temperature	75° F-85° F	Mild Fruit	Mild Fruit	Lt. Clove	Mild Fruit	Banana
		Clean	Clean	Bubblegum	Clean	Vanilla
		Malt	Slightly Tart	Banana	Malt	Lt. Clove
			Malt	Alcohol		Bubble Gum
				Fruity		Fruity
				Fruity		Fruity
	65° F-75° F	Clean	Clean	Clove	Clean	Banana
		Lt. Lager	Lt. Lager	Alcohol	Lt. Lager	Vanilla
		Sulfur	Sulfur	Phenolic	Sulfur	Clove
		Lt. Fruit	Lt. Fruit	Fruity	Lt. Fruit	Sulfur
			Slightly Tart	Lt. Banana		
Beer Styles	*Weizen/ Weissbier*					✓
	Dunkelweizen					✓
	Weizenbock					✓
	Witbier			✓		
	American Wheat	✓	✓		✓	
	Berliner *Weisse*	✓	✓		✓	
	Lambic/ Gueuze					

*Limited availability through seasonal release.
Notes to brewers:
1. All of these descriptions are based on standard pitch rates, oxygenation levels, and brewing practices.
2. Increasing pitch rates will decrease ester (fruit) profile.

Wyeast Laboratories Wheat Strains

Wyeast Strain Number		3068	3191*	3278	3333	3463
Wyeast Strain Name		Weihen-stephan Weizen	Berliner-Weisse Blend	Lambic Blend	German Wheat	Forbidden Fruit
Flocculation		Low	Low	NA	High	Low
Attenuation %		73-77	75-77	NA	70-76	72-76
Alcohol Tolerance % by Weight		10	10	12	10	12
Temperature	75° F-85° F	Banana	Tart	Sour	Banana	Clove
		Lt. Clove	Fruity	Earthy	Lt. Clove	Fruity
		Bubble Gum	Earthy	Fruity	Bubble Gum	Tart
		Fruity	Acidic	Phenolic	Fruity	Banana
				Barnyard		Phenolic
				Pie Cherry		Phenolic
	65° F-75° F	Banana	Tart	Sour	Banana	Clove
		Clove	Earthy	Earthy	Clove	Tart
		Bubble Gum	Lt. Fruit	Fruity	Bubble Gum	Phenolic
		Fruity	Acidic	Phenolic	Fruity	Fruity
		Sulfur		Barnyard		Sulfur
				Pie Cherry		
Beer Styles	Weizen/ Weissbier	✓			✓	
	Dunkelweizen	✓			✓	
	Weizenbock	✓			✓	
	Witbier					✓
	American Wheat		✓			
	Berliner Weisse					
	Lambic/ Gueuze			✓		

Wyeast Laboratories Wheat Strains

Wyeast Strain Number		3638	3763*	3942	3944
Wyeast Strain Name		Bavarian Wheat	Roeselare	Belgian Wheat	Belgian *Witbier*
Flocculation		Low	NA	Medium	Med-High
Attenuation %		70-76	NA	72-76	72-76
Alcohol Tolerance % by Weight		10	12	12	11-12
Temperature	75° F-85° F	Banana	Sour	Clove	Clove
		Vanilla	Earthy	Lt. Solvent	Phenolic
		Lt. Clove	Fruity	Banana	Lt. Banana
		Bubble Gum	Phenolic	Fruity	Tart
		Fruity	Barnyard	Phenolic	
		Fruity	Pie Cherry	Phenolic	
	65° F-75° F	Banana	Sour	Lt. Clove	Clove
		Vanilla	Earthy	Yeasty	Phenolic
		Clove	Fruity	Banana	Lt. Tart
		Sulfur	Phenolic	Fruity	Sulfur
			Barnyard	Sulfur	
			Pie Cherry		
Beer Styles	*Weizen/ Weissbier*	✓			
	Dunkelweizen	✓			
	Weizenbock	✓			
	Witbier			✓	✓
	American Wheat				
	Berliner *Weisse*				
	Lambic/ Gueuze		✓		

BIBLIOGRAPHY

Anderson, Will. *The Beer Book*. Philadelphia: Pyne Press, 1973.

Annemüller, Gerolf, Hans-J. Manger, and Peter Lietz. *Die Berliner Weisse: Ein Stück Berliner Geschichte*. Berlin: VLBFachbücher, 2008.

Arnold, John P. *Origin and History of Beer and Brewing From Prehistoric Times to the Beginning of Brewing Science and Technology*. Chicago: Alumni Association of the Wahl-Henius Institute of Fermentology, 1911. Reprint. BeerBooks.com, 2005.

Back, Werner. *Ausgewählte Kapitel der Brauereitechnologie*. Nürnberg: Carl, 2005.

Bentley, Richard, et al., *Bentley's Miscellany, Vol. 46*. London: Richard Bentley, 1859.

Casey, Gregory. "Origins and Controlling Esters and Higher Alcohols in Beer." Presentation at Rocky Mountain Microbrewing Symposium, Colorado Springs, Colo., 2005.

Celis, Pierre. *My Life*. Antwerp, Belgium: Media Marketing Communications, 2005.

Coppinger, Joseph. *The American Practical Brewer and Tanner.* New York: Van Winkle and Wiley, 1815.

Cornell, Martyn. *Amber, Gold, and Black: The History of Britain's Great Beers.* London: The History Press, 2010.

Corran, H.S. *A History of Brewing.* London: David & Charles, 1975.

Daniels, Ray. *Designing Great Beers.* Boulder, Colo.: Brewers Publications, 1996.

Daniels, Ray, and Geoffrey Larson. *Smoked Beers.* Boulder, Colo: Brewers Publications, 2000.

Davison, Dennis. "Inside Berlin's Beer." *Zymurgy* 19, no. 4 (Winter 1996), 36-41.

De Clerck, Jean. *Cours de Brasserie.* Leuven, Belgium: Van Linthout, 1948.

———— *Cours de Brasserie* (2nd edition). Leuven, Belgium: UCL, 1962.

Depraetere, S., F. Delvaux, S. Coghel, and F.R. Delvaux. "Wheat Variety and Barley Malt Properties: Influence on Haze Intensity and Foam Stability of Wheat Beer," *Journal of Institute of Brewing* 110, no. 3 (2004), 200-206.

Delvaux, F., F. Combes, and F.R. Delvaux. "The Effect of Wheat Malting on Colloidal Haze of White Beers." *Master Brewers Association Technical Quarterly* 41, no. 1 (2004), 27-32.

"Different Weiss Beers." *The Western Brewer: and Journal of the Barley, Malt, and Hop Trades* (July 15, 1900): 282.

Frentz, Adolphe. *Livre de Poche du Fabricant de Bière Blanche*. Brussels: Laurent, 1872.

Grant, Bert with Robert Spector. *The Ale Master*. Seattle: Sasquatch Books, 1998.

Hornsey, Ian. *A History of Beer and Brewing*. Cambridge, England: Royal Society of Chemistry, 2003.

Hoverson, Doug. *Land of Amber Waters: The History of Brewing in Minnesota*. Minneapolis: University of Minnesota Press, 2007.

Jackson, Michael. "Going for Gose." *The Beer Hunter*. Available at http://beerhunter.com/documents/19133-001353.html.

————. *The Great Beers of Belgium*. 5th ed. London: Prion Books, 2001.

————. *Michael Jackson's Beer Companion*. Philadelphia: Running Press, 1993.

————. *The New World Guide to Beer*. Philadelphia: Running Press, 1988.

————. *The Pocket Guide to Beer*. New York: Perigee Books, 1982.

————. *The Running Press Pocket Guide to Beer*. Philadelphia: Running Press, 2000.

————. "Salty trail of Germany's link with wild beer." *The Beer Hunter*. Available at http://beerhunter.com/documents/19133-000844.html.

————. *World Guide to Beer*. London: Quarto, 1977.

Jacob, H.E. *Six Thousand Years of Bread*. Garden City, N.Y.: Doubleday, Doran, and Co., 1944.

Kious, K., H. Herbst, and D. Roussin. *St. Louis Brews: 200 Years of Brewing in St. Louis, 1809-2009*. St. Louis: Reedy Press, 2009.

Kitsock, Greg. "Celis and Spice: A Beer With an International Following." *Zymurgy* 23, no. 3 (May-June 2000), 43-46.

Kuplent, Florian. "Berliner Weissbier," *BrewingTechniques* 7, no. 1 (January-February 1999), 26-33.

Lacambre, G. *Traité Complet de la Fabrication des Bières et de la Distillation des Grains*. Brussels: Decq, 1851.

Laurent, Auguste. *Dictionnaire de Brasserie*. Brussels: Laurent, 1875.

Levesque, John. *The Art of Brewing and Fermenting*. London: Thomas Hurst, 1836.

Lodahl, Martin. "Witbier: Belgian White," *BrewingTechniques* 2, no. 4 (July-August 1994), 24-27.

Logsdon, Dave, Dave Bryant, and Larry Nielsen. "Wheat Beer Flavor From Thirteen Different Yeasts in Head-to-Head Competition." Presentation at the Craft Brewers Conference, New Orleans, 2003.

Miller, Carl. *Breweries of Cleveland*. Cleveland: Schnitzelbank Press, 1998.

Mosher, Randy. *The Brewer's Companion*. Seattle: Alephenalia Publications, 1995.

————. *Radical Brewing*. Boulder, Colo.: Brewers Publications, 2004.

Nitschke, R. "Traditional Production of Wheat Beer—from the Small Brewery to the Market Leader." *Master Brewers Association of the Americas Technical Quarterly* 32, no. 3 (1995), 147-151.

Ockert, Karl, editor. *MBAA Practical Handbook for the Specialty Brewer.* Vol. 2: *Fermentation, Cellaring, and Packaging Operations.* St. Paul, Minn.: Master Brewers Association of the Americas, 2006.

Pattinson, Ronald. *Decoction!* Amsterdam: Kilderkin, 2008.

Pelset, N. *Traité Théorique et Pratique de la Fabrication de la Grisette et des Bières Pales.* Brussels: Laurent, 1874.

Perrier-Robert, Annie, and Charles Fontaine. *Belgium By Beer, Beer By Belgium.* Luxembourg: Schortgen, Esch/Alzette, 1996.

Rajotte, Pierre. *Belgian Ale.* Boulder, Colo.: Brewers Publications, 1992.

Sparrow, Jeff. "Cloudy With a Chance for Haze: The History and Brewing Techniques of Belgian Witbier," *Zymurgy* 25, no. 3 (May/June 2002), 26-33.

————— "Going Sour on German Beer," *Zymurgy* 24, no. 4 (July-August 2001), 20-25.

Thausing, Julius, Anton Schwarz, and A.H. Bauer. *Theory and Practice of the Preparation of Malt and the Fabrication of Beer.* Philadelphia: Henry Carey Baird & Co., 1882. Reprint. BeerBooks.com, 2007.

Unger, Richard. *Beer in the Middle Ages and Renaissance.* Philadelphia: University of Pennsylvania Press, 2004.

Vanbeneden, N., T.V. Roey, F. Willems, F. Delvaux, and F.R. Delvaux. "Formation of 4-Vinyl and 4-Ethyl Derivatives From Hydroxycinnamic Acids: Occurrence of Volatile Phenolic Flavour Compounds in Beer and Distribution of Pad1-Activity Among Brewing Yeasts," *Food Chemistry* 107 (2008), 221-230.

—————. "Release of Phenolic Flavour Precursors During Wort Production: Influence of Process Parameters and Grist Composition on Ferulic Acid Release During Brewing." *Food Chemistry* 111 (2008), 83-91.

Vanderstichele, G. *La Brasserie de Fermentation Haute*. Turnhout, Belgium: Splichat Joseph, 1905.

Verlinden, Hendrik. *Leerboek der Gistingsnijverheid*. Self-published, 1933.

Vermeylen, Joseph. *Traité de la Fabrication du Malt et de la Bière*. Ghent, Belgium: Institut Supérior des Fermentations, 1962.

Vrancken, Jean-Baptiste. *Sur la Bière*. Rotterdam, The Netherlands: Van Baalen, 1829.

Vizetelly, Henry. *Berlin Under the New Empire*. London: Tinsley Brothers, 1879.

Wagner, Rich. "Philadelphia Weiss Beer Brewers." *American Breweriana Journal*, no. 159 (May-June 2009).

Wahl, Robert and Max Henius, *American Handy Book of the Brewing, Malting, and Auxiliary Trades*. Chicago: Wahl & Henius, 1901.

Warner, Eric. *German Wheat Beer*. Boulder, Colo.: Brewers Publications, 1992.

Webb, Tim and Joris Pattyn. *100 Belgian Beers to Try Before You Die!* St. Albans, England: CAMRA Books, 2008.

"What Weiss Beer Is." *The Western Brewer: and Journal of the Barley, Malt, and Hop Trades* (March 15, 1882): 889.

INDEX